Death Shall Have
No Dominion

Death Shall Have No Dominion

A New Testament Study

Douglas T. Holden

THE BETHANY PRESS

ST. LOUIS, MISSOURI

Distributed by The G. R. Welch Company, Toronto, Ontario,
Canada. Other foreign distribution by Feffer and Simons, Inc.,
New York, New York.

MANUFACTURED IN THE UNITED STATES OF AMERICA

To My Parents

who have given me βίος
that I may have Ζωή

Acknowledgments

I count it a high privilege and a great personal pleasure to have had numerous people share a portion of their lives with me in this venture. I am especially grateful to Professor Edgar P. Dickie, M.C., D.D., D.Litt., Emeritus Professor of Divinity of St. Mary's College, the University of St. Andrews; to Professor Matthew Black, D.D., D.Litt., D.Theol., F.B.A., Professor of Divinity and Biblical Criticism, and Principal of St. Mary's College, the University of St. Andrews; and to my secretary, Mrs. Arthur V. Sewell, of Bartow, Florida. I shall always be exceedingly thankful for their lives and mindful of their kind and generous contributions to this work.

I would be remiss in my acknowledgments without listing several who have added greatly to my work. Each will know in his own way why he or she is presently held up. I simply list them: Mrs. Walter M. Holden, Mrs. A. J. Stevens, Mr. Max Wells Holden, Dr. Merrill R. Abbey, Rev. Mr. John R. W. Stott, Dr. Russell L. Dicks, Dr. John W. Carlton, Rev. Mr. Dayle G. Groh, Rev. Mr. Jacob C. Martinson, Dr. George A. Foster, Mr. and Mrs. John H. Paterson, Mr. and Mrs. Carter S. Roberts, Dr. Charles T. Thrift, Jr., Miss Jeanette Kampen, and Dr. Howard E. Short. My life has been enriched and ennobled by their lives.

7

Contents

Introduction

DEATH is the most offensive subject confronting contemporary man. Our society, like that of the Greeks of old, is so threatened by the inevitability of death and the failure to believe that there is anything beyond, that man evades death through frantic self-indulgence. Anything which might imply that man must eventually die places an immense question mark before him that negates all his values. Man would rather die than think about death. Death is no longer seen as a portal opening to a greater life but rather as a wall in which there is "no exit." If one mentions the word *death* in polite society, he is considered to be obscene. Perhaps history will distinguish this century by defining it as a "death-denying" culture.

There is a conspiracy of silence shrouding concepts of death. A child's first encounter with religion may be through his attitudes toward, or his knowledge of, death. It is dismissed all too soon; the fact that a child can grasp a concept of death as readily as can an adult is not taken into account. Children may first pray:

> If I should die before I wake,
> I pray the Lord my soul to take.

Although a parent might be quite willing to teach this simple prayer, a death in the family will evoke an entirely different response. The child is usually not permitted to attend the funeral and is often euphemistically told anything, with the exception that the person did in fact die.

A person may go through life without ever discussing the topic of death in any depth and thus find himself ill-equipped to face it intellectually, emotionally, or spiritually. The offense of death frequently leaves the bereaved alone to work out his grief since there are so few who are willing to share with him or to talk with him meaningfully about death. The horror of death usually isolates the dying from their friends and relatives. The process of dying is "managed" in institutions by professionals in a remote and impersonal manner. The prospect of dying at home in bed surrounded by one's family is indeed highly improbable. The individual is frequently denied the privilege of being conscious at his own death. Tolstoi believed death to be the most significant event in life. It is very possible that this is a time of the greatest religious crisis and impact. The church is often excluded from sharing with the dying when it alone can offer consolation and meaning.

Sociologists continually assert that life has changed drastically since World War II; many never realize that death too has changed. During the medieval period man prayed for a lingering death so that he could be prepared to meet the Christ of judgment. Today's man has completely inverted this desire, for he feels that death is so grim that one need not prolong the agony. The sudden, unexpected death, which is usually called "untimely" or "accidental," is rapidly becoming standard. Though medical science has made great strides in pushing back the time of death, there is little that medicine can do to check the increasing number of violent deaths. Wars, bombings, prison camps, and automobiles have done much to change the strategy of death. Soon the accidental or violent death will be listed in the obituaries as one resulting from "natural causes." The suddenness of death is usually thought to be a blessing in disguise because the deceased is removed from reflection on, and preparation for, death. In the future the increased mobility of life may in fact preclude any prediction of the advent of death for the individual. It would seem then that the wise man would be prepared to meet death at any juncture.

The study of death is as awesome as it is threatening. Since the problem of death will remain intellectually insoluble, it will probably never gain the unlimited attention of philosophers and theologians. Philosophy has stepped lightly around the subject because many philosophers have dismissed it as a proper subject for their inquiries. Death has been relegated to the field of biology, to be studied as an organic process, or to psychology, where it is considered to be our "basic anxiety." Since death strikes the totality of man, it calls for a concerted effort of all disciplines related to man. Interest in death per se diminished with the rise of Christian eschatology and its promise of eternal life. With the failure of the church to make these doctrines relevant for this age, other disciplines have opened the door to speculation and research on the meaning of death.

Death continues to raise many ethical problems which have profound religious implications. Such problems as suicide, abortion, euthanasia, cryogenics, heart transplants, grief, and basic honesty with terminal patients are pressing for answers. These questions have been dealt with basically from a legal standpoint though they are fundamentally theological in origin. Should a Christian family established on love and honesty deceive the dying one at the end? What consolation does the church have to offer the bereaved? Does not the church have an attitude toward the practice of euthanasia and abortion? What will happen to Christian eschatology if the individual can be rejuvenated after being frozen?

These are some of the questions that cry out for insight. The church can begin to answer them only when theologians attempt to discover what is the meaning of life and death. The path is long and difficult, but perhaps it is the most important and most necessary inquiry in our time. If the church does not soon speak to these issues with wisdom and insight, it will lose the opportunity to speak at all. Certainly the Christian church, of all the institutions, should be able to face death.

With the implications of the problem of death pressing relentlessly upon the church, there is much groundwork to be done. The theologian is so often engrossed in theological detail that he forgets people die daily. It is an answer to these practical problems that society demands of theology. The great task before the church is to find out what it really has to say in regard to death. What is death? What does the death of Christ mean? What are the implications of the death of Christ for the individual believer? All these questions are primary and fundamental for the completion of the Christian perspective toward death.

It would seem that the Christian perspective has become more obscure over the years. What the church saw so clearly and proclaimed so forcefully has become fuzzy and vague. Christian theology has become so fused with Greek philosophy that it has reared individuals who are a mixture of nine parts Greek thought to one part Christian thought. Thus the church on any given Sunday is more likely to proclaim immortality than resurrection. It can no longer affirm a creed that gives assent to victory over death and yet find itself speechless when confronted by death. The church's silence on the issues of death has caused the majority of people since World War II to find the meaning and purpose of life and death outside the confines of its walls. The church was not unscathed by warfare—more individuals died for the sake of Christ in this century than in all previous centuries combined. The cost of discipleship, which is often extravagant today, promises that martyrdom is not simply a relic of the early church. Is the church to reply that these lives were given in vain? If it dares to ask individuals to hold the faith even in death, should not the church have the courage in peaceful times to establish what it believes about death?

The topics raised here are deep and searching. No man could attempt to answer all of them. It will take the prolonged devotion of many dedicated men to reach even a tentative formulation. The task is not hopeless, however, because it is God who has given death meaning and it is he who bids us to come. Individuals come to the church seeking answers to their problems with death. The church must stand ready to meet them, with the realization that it was born out of death and that it is Christ who has ultimately changed the meaning of death. Thus man should come to the church to find the meaning of both life and death, for the Christian message speaks directly to both.

This life is shared with death; if one is realistic, the whole of life must be thought out in terms of death. The fact of death alone gives true depth to the question of the meaning of life. It is from the perspective of death that the Christian learns to live. One learns to value every moment, thought, and deed as if it were the last. One learns to trust God in death as he has in life. For if man is not prepared to die today, certainly he will not be prepared to die tomorrow. If he is not prepared to live today, how can he expect to be prepared to live tomorrow?

In order to find where the church stands today, one must first discern where it stood in the past. The writings of the church have frequently concerned the subject of death; therefore, the church has a theology of death that is implicit in all its writings but has become repressed with time. The task is monumental but absolutely necessary. A religion that has as its theme the death of its Founder and his subsequent victory over it must inevitably address itself to the meaning of death. For it is because of Christ's meaningful death that the church can speak to the death of all men. Any failure to do so ultimately weakens Christianity at its strongest point. To remove, to belittle, or to deny the Christian beliefs concerning death is to disembowel the church and to cause the whole superstructure of the church to come tumbling down. Failure to speak to death realistically and unashamedly is in fact a denial of Christianity.

It was by no means conceived that this one writing could answer all the questions concerning Christian beliefs in regard to death. The theme presented here is a survey of New Testament thought which demonstrates the basic attitudes toward death in the New Testament writings. No Christian perspective could be found without dealing with the fundamental concepts herein. This book is simply a start, but nevertheless it is a basic start. All of Christian theology is related to the death of Christ, so it is to his death that the church must continually readdress itself. If the church is bold enough to hold before the world the symbol of a crucified Savior, could it not also have the audacious spirit to "proclaim the Lord's death until he comes"?

1

The Concept of Death
in the
Synoptic Gospels

The word they preached was the very thing
which had once made them afraid to speak.
                                    —James Denney

THE inevitable question of death raised its ugly head rapidly within the early church. The concept of death was no longer answered by a logical extension of the love, the power, and the justice of God, but rather it was answered by a direct result of the emphasis on Christ's teachings and resurrection. The resurrection of Christ gave substance for profound speculation, which must have provoked discussions and opened ramifications far beyond those proposed by the Jewish rabbis. Eschatology in a real sense had been uprooted and replanted from a point completely outside human history into the very center of men's lives and activities. The resurrection for the Jews would come during "the Day" in the distant future, but now it presented itself before their eyes and within their hearts. The kingdom of God, the resurrection, and judgment focused on the humdrum of daily existence. Man could no longer put these questions aside as he had formerly done, because they drew near with terrifying intimacy. Surely, the "last things" had now been placed first, for in a real sense the world had been turned

17

upside down. The conversion of the world began with inversion of the world—it all pivoted on the resurrection of Christ.

It was sincerely and hopefully felt that this same Jesus, who had somehow returned from the very jaws of death, would come again in the immediate future and draw these faithful individuals to himself, hopefully while they lived. Thus, every day was eked out under the anxiety of waiting and the anticipation of the end of hopeful longings. However, in a much more practical way, the hard reality of death continued to take the lives of the faithful, and thus the church had to address itself to this very pressing question which challenged the meaning, purpose, and nature of Christ's resurrection. The very foundation of Christianity was under attack. The meaning of the resurrection had to be dealt with not only for those outside the church, who used the resurrection for the aperture to attack, but especially for the believers who had made the resurrection the core and crux of their conviction and the spark that kindled their message. In outward appearance the death of a Christian was no different from the death of any other individual. Again and again the question arose as to what in fact was to happen to Christians when they died.

The concept of death in New Testament times came in a much more "natural" way than it was to be received by succeeding generations of Western civilization. By "natural," the implication is made that death was very common to everyday experience and frequently occurred early in life. Thus, the whole aspect of death must be seen from the "naturalness" which remains behind every human death.

In the time of Jesus, mortality rates were high and life expectancy was low. Those Jews who were able to avoid numerous diseases were subject to the numerous and frequently bizarre cruelties of their foreign conquerors. Untimely and unexpected death was a constant threat. Certainly as a far greater menace to life and as a far more frequent visitor than we can realize, death came to take a more active part in the thought, the liturgy, the social customs, and generally in the whole gamut of Jewish life. There was no evasion or suppression of either the fact or the reality of death; rather, it was

18

dealt with in a straightforward manner. Of all the admirable factors in the Hebrew faith that one might hold up, perhaps the finest is the fact that death was confronted as a reality to be met openly and honestly. But beyond the horrible, grim realities, the Hebrews began to see fulfillment which pointed to a beyond. This came as a result of dealing with death squarely, not denying it or belittling it. This honesty in seeking led the Hebrews to their most profound thoughts of God, such as those found in Job, Genesis, and the Psalms, and such as those revealed by the Prophets. Theological insight came not as a claim or demand upon God but rather as a breakthrough into his nature. Here, then, was the foundation for Jesus' teachings concerning death and ultimately the understanding of his death and resurrection.

In the time of Jesus it was not an uncommon sight to see children acting out funerals in much the same manner as our young people may play their games. Yet, society was not offended by this nor were the children thwarted in such activities. Jesus compared that generation to a group of children playing and yelling to one another:

> "We piped to you, and you did not dance;
> we wailed, and you did not mourn."
> —Matthew 11:17; Luke 7:32

Just as the children were uninhibited in their thoughts of death, so too were the adults. In the records of Jesus' ministry there are numerous statements relating to death as well as many questions regarding it asked by those who sought him out. Obviously death was continually on their minds; they spoke openly about it and hence were not rebuked. The mere frankness of their speech indicates a much healthier attitude toward death than we exhibit in our culture.

The Gospel of Matthew begins by telling of Jesus' narrow escape from death as a babe (Matt. 2:7-23). No doubt this ability to seek out and destroy children not only reflected the nature of the Roman Empire but also suggested that life could be counted as nothing. It was under this reign of terror that Jesus had to work out his life and ministry. Also, it is of interest to see that the writer presents this in an objective manner, which is indicative that these killings were rather common or that the bold story should stand by itself. Jesus' nature and destiny from the earliest sources connote the imminence of death. The shadow of death hung large and longingly over all his travels, teachings, and healings. It was not until the death of Herod that Jesus' family felt safe enough to return to Nazareth.

The life of the individual in these times was very unstable and insecure. The innocent had as much to fear as the criminal. John the Baptist was shamefully killed by Herod the Tetrarch because of a woman's whims. This story brings home a convincing reminder of the frailty and transience of life. Always this must be borne in mind when we look at the Gospels.

Again and again there are accounts of violent deaths in the teachings of Jesus. There is the parable of the wicked tenants (Matt. 21:33-43) and the parable of the marriage of the king's son in which the wedding guests displayed their hate for the king by killing his messengers (Matt. 22:2-10). These stories would gain significance only if the facts were true. No doubt these were only a few examples from which Jesus could draw in order to reveal the stark brutality of the times.

Violence and murder were so commonplace that Jesus warned any would-be followers of the possible disastrous results (Matt. 23:34). Death for Jesus' disciples could well be the very cost of discipleship.

Violent death at this point in history was always thought to be doled out to men for their wickedness. The thought behind the story in Luke 13:1-5 is that men shall die in the same manner in which they have lived. It is the same problem Job wrestled with centuries before as he sought to match his sins with his punishment. He had to conclude that the wicked often prosper and frequently die in both peace and affluence. The basic theme behind these stories and the parable of the unfruitful fig tree (Luke 13:6-9) is the clear and urgent call to repentance.

There is no indication that these violent deaths had anything to do with moral status. While numerous theories may be given as to why these questions were proposed, it can only safely be assumed that men sought what they believed was God's will in these contemporary examples. They were asking the same questions that the Book of Job raised or the disciples when they saw the man who was blind from birth (John 9). Jesus did not attempt to expound a philosophy of evil. He merely corrected the error of men's thinking that these tragedies were related to wickedness and moved on to a call for repentance so that they might not perish, but rather find wholeness (salvation).

Wherever one may begin a system of eschatology, he must interpret the kingdom of God and its meaning for Jesus. It is true that the Jews awaited a messianic kingdom to come in glory and in power on earth. This idea would not be put down, yet there continued a growing awareness that earthly imperfections made the earth an unsuitable place for such a kingdom. The Jewish answer to this problem resolved itself for the time being by maintaining that the kingdom would come on earth for a temporary period, and then it would be fulfilled and consummated fully and finally in heaven. Here also was found the breakdown of national hopes of salvation, for the kingdom would not be synonymous with the nation Israel but rather would be built by the remnant few who had been faithful. Thus, the Jewish religion turned from one based on nationalism to one based on individualism. The individual from the time of Jeremiah and Ezekiel became the most important factor in their religion and, rightly or wrongly, it has been carried on through contemporary Christianity.

R. H. Charles maintains that within the teachings of Jesus was the true synthesis of the two concepts of the kingdom of God.

By the Founder of Christianity, however, the synthesis of the two hopes was established in a universal form finally and for ever. The true Messianic kingdom begins on earth, and will be consummated in heaven; it is not temporary, but eternal; it is not limited to one people, but embraces the righteous of all nations and of all times. It forms a divine society in which the position and significance of each member is determined by his endowments, and his blessedness conditioned by the blessedness of the whole. Thus religious individualism becomes an impossibility.[1]

The eschatology of a nation is always the last part of their religion to experience the transforming power of new ideas and new facts.[2]

One cannot assume that even Jesus could have lifted and changed all the incompatible irregularities and unharmonious elements in the Jewish religion. Even had he done so, these problems would have crept in again by those who handed down his teachings to us. Jesus stood in basic agreement with the theology of the Old Testament and essentially he did not attempt to change it. His task was one of reformation, that is, of taking the people of Israel back to the truths of God. It is quite apparent that the majority of the Jews were so far removed from the Scriptures that they could no longer uphold what they once vowed to live by, and so they came to violent disagreements with Jesus. Further insights into their religion no doubt would have driven a wider gap in their thoughts. Thus, much of the Old Testament teaching comes over *in toto* to the religion of the New Testament.[3]

Christ was the first member of the new community of Christians *to face death*. While it is easy for scholars to point out that his death was unique, it was not necessarily maintained by the early Christians that their deaths should be in any way different. No doubt there was much confusion at this point because full or complete understanding was lacking. Though the Pharisees had taught resurrection, the appearances of Jesus added innovations to this old concept. Long before the doctrines of the church took shape, the deaths of confessing Christians challenged the faith of those left behind. Stephen and James were among the very first to die. What was to be their outcome? The early followers accepted that in some vague sense they were with the Lord, yet how were they really to know their status or condition?

In addition to these perplexing questions there was the problem of an ever-growing number who had heard the Christian gospel preached to them but made no effort to respond. Perhaps even more serious was the problem of those who began to believe and follow but then turned back. This is dramatically and terrifyingly presented in the account of Ananias and Sapphira, who were deemed unworthy disciples. They, according to C. Ryder Smith, "would pass into a different state—not, however, because they had sinned, but because they refused to be saved from sin."[4] What, then, was the consequence of not fulfilling the faith one proclaimed? No doubt this covered a wide range of people who had been challenged by the Christian message but had turned their backs on it. These individuals were to be found in the same state as all sinners according to contemporary Jewish thought.

Then, of course, there was that persistent problem of many living in "the far corners of the earth," who had not been encountered by the disciples, not to mention the God-fearing and the ungodly who had lived and died before the Christ event. These people were dealt with in the completely moral way which had evolved at the time of the New Testament. The good would be subject to blessing and the wicked would be punished. The punishment might range from a dismal state of existence to physical torture. Basically, we see that the Old Testament concepts continued, but there were many doubts and uncertainties about what really happened to the individual. And certainly people were perplexed by two questions: What difference does Christ's death make? What is the whole point and purpose of Christianity?

As for the actual state of the dead, the believers also continued to follow closely along the line of Old Testament beliefs. At the juncture of death man disintegrated into the three elements which, when combined, make man man. This trichotomy appears in 1 Thessalonians 5:23. There is no clear distinction as to what happens to the three elements, for though they themselves are often diffused the basic trichotomy continues. Man is the integration of "body," "soul," and "spirit," but when he passes into the intermediate state these three constituting factors are dismantled. Every man, regardless of his moral condition, has to undergo this fragmentation according to Hebrew thought, for these parts are necessary to make a whole man. Thus, the inference is made that man at death is always something less than whole.

Man at the instant of death parts with his "psyche" (soul). However, for the Christian the "psyche" is maintained in safe-keeping under the watchful eye of the Creator, who will re-embody it at the Parousia. The souls of men are separated to enter Hades, except for the soul of Jesus, who was not abandoned to Hades (Acts 2:31). Hades stands for the immediate position of the soul but not the final place.

What, then, is to become of the "spirit" of the dead? There is here no difference between the two Testaments. Early Hebrew thought maintained that man was a dichotomy of "soul" and "body." During the period of the Exile man evolved from a dichotomy to a trichotomy, with the addition of a "spirit" which first appears in the Book of Enoch. The "spirit" continues to maintain its individuality and take on form unrelated to its earthly body. Jesus said, "Father, into thy hands I commit my spirit!" (Luke 23:46). The whole tradition of the church has been that certainly God did receive his spirit. Also, it is recorded that Stephen asked in his prayer, "Lord Jesus, receive my spirit" (Acts 7:59). The spirit of the good thus goes to be with God, and the spirit of the evil goes to prison (1 Peter 3:19). This concept of the prison also comes from the Book of Enoch (chap. 67).

The body was not so difficult to understand because, due to open family tombs, the dead were seen in all stages of decomposition. In the Hebrew religion the body had to be put away or buried to preserve the dignity of the individual. Also, it was maintained that the corpse was itself unclean and defiled those who dealt with it, as in the account of the Good Samaritan. However, the thought pattern of the Hebrew was such that when he referred to the burial of the individual he meant only the body. This body was destructible, for it was corruptible. Except for the body of Jesus, the New Testament merely reiterates Old Testament concepts of the body.

It is therefore quite wrong to infer that the whole of a man passes into the intermediate state. One disintegrates into three separate forms at death, each part having its own fate. However, it becomes very confusing because each part may be referred to by a personal name or pronoun. The New Testament merely engulfs the Old Testament trichotomy and adds to it the concept of dying and being with Christ, which is only a modification of the older thought.

The concept of the dead being asleep is also present in the New Testament. It stems from the sameness of sleep and death in outward appearance. The idea continued from Old Testament times and even lingers on today, no doubt because of the restful and peaceful appearance of both. This term *sleep* can be used for all the dead, but it is usually reserved for the good who have died. Although which aspect of the individual actually slept was never stressed, the implication was that it was both soul and body.[5]

Jesus used the term *paradise* in his answer to the plea of the man on the cross. Jesus stated that that very day the man would enter paradise with him, which by implication meant that he would simply be present with Jesus. Paradise itself has many synonyms; Luke uses "eternal habitations" and "Abraham's bosom." The implication of these is the expression of nearness to God. Out of these passages no more definite teaching concerning paradise may be drawn.

In the Gospels themselves there is just this one passage in Luke to consider, the statement made to the dying thief (Luke 23:43). Sometimes paradise is viewed as the intermediate abode of the righteous, as in 1 Enoch 60:8—61:12; on other occasions it means an eternal abode, as in 2 Enoch 8:9; 42:3; 61:3; 65:10; 2(4) Esdras 7:36, 123; 8:52. Jesus could have implied either meaning when he spoke these words. One should not conjecture very much about them because the cross was obviously no place to develop a theology of the hereafter. He gave complete assurance to the thief, in words that held meaning for him, that he would be with God and with Jesus.

In heaven the righteous and the angels dwell with God. Thus, Jesus addresses God as the Father "who art in heaven" (Matt. 6:9) and again as "my Father who is in heaven" (Matt. 10:33). He also declares that the angels of the little ones always "behold the face of my Father who is in heaven" (Matt. 18:

10). Heaven was the abode of Jesus before his descent to earth, and there he returned when his redemptive work was completed (Luke 24:51). The final abode with God in heaven prevails in the New Testament. Jesus speaks of the time when he will appear from heaven and will gather together his elect (Matt. 24:30-31; Mark 13:26-27; Luke 21:27). In heaven his disciples will enjoy a great reward (Matt. 5:12; Luke 6:23). They are urged to lay up "treasures" in heaven (Matt. 6:20).

Before one can come to any understanding or reach any conclusions with regard to the concept of death in the Synoptic Gospels, he will have to look carefully at those passages which deal specifically with death. In the Gospel of Luke is found the famous *Nunc Dimittis* passage (2:25-35). This is the first recorded encounter that Jesus had with the thought of death. Simeon is regarded as a saintly and elderly man by implication, who waited patiently in the temple area for the coming of the Messiah. By some mysterious revelation through the Holy Spirit, he was informed that he would not see death until he had seen the Lord's Christ (anointed one). Although it is generally assumed that Simeon was a very old man, this is not, however, necessarily true. In fact, there is nothing said in the account about Simeon's age. Readers draw this conclusion because of lack of careful examination. No doubt many confuse this story with the following story of the prophetess Anna, who was, the text tells us, "of a great age" (Luke 2:36).

The other error is the assumption that Simeon saw Jesus and died.[6] It is easy to think that this man, who had waited about the temple during his lengthy life for the long-awaited Messiah, died after seeing him. In actual fact the scripture tells us only that at last his life was fulfilled because he had seen Jesus. Afterward Simeon was prepared to meet death at any point because his encounter with the living God had made life complete. This, of course, is true of all Christian experience, yet to encounter God does not mean death, for it is only then that one can fulfill life.

The Greek word 'Aπολύω used here means "to set free or release"; thus, Jesus could say to the crippled woman, "Woman, you are freed [or released] from your infirmity"

(Luke 13:12).[7] Simeon found a sense of release, or achievement, or fulfillment of life which an encounter with Christ involves. While this does not enter the concept of death itself, the peace and confidence present here are not limited to this life. This insight came to Simeon not as release from a burden but as a release to achievement and fulfillment of life. Although this does not probe the meaning of death, it shows that this encounter opened him to a new depth and richness of experience which gave new meaning to both life and death. The high point of Simeon's life *was to see Jesus* because it was only through Jesus that Simeon was able to satisfy his longing. And because life then became full, complete, and meaningful through the sight of Jesus, it was possible to resign himself to the fact of death, which ultimately meant to be with Jesus. So one concludes that Simeon did not die upon seeing Jesus, but rather that he continued to live in a new sense of being "in peace." He could say that he truly lived "in peace" and died "in peace." It was this new unity of life with death that transcended all other demissions and made Christianity unique.

Perhaps no passage has been more difficult to understand than the famous *Crux Interpretum* (Mark 9:1; Matt. 16:28; Luke 9:27). The Markan passage reads, ". . . there are some standing here who will not taste death before they see the kingdom of God come with power." This is one of the most difficult passages of eschatology.[8]

We know in retrospect that the kingdom did not come in as it was expected. Further, those who were standing there did in fact experience death. The conclusion that one has to draw is the fact that Jesus was mistaken in regard to the imminence of the kingdom. But one cannot solve the problem of whether Jesus was misunderstood or whether he himself was actually mistaken about the time of the end.

Our special interest being the interpretation of the meaning of death, we can conclude that Jesus was thinking of death as an inevitable event, not far distant, but equally not in the immediate future. It is possible that the particular phrase "taste of death" owes something to the connexion with Elijah, through 4 Ezra;

but this connexion does not require that Jesus was here promising that some of his hearers would never die.[9]

There are two graphic illustrations of Jesus' confrontations with death in the Synoptic Gospels. These are the case of the daughter of Jairus and the case of the son of the widow of Nain. Both will be considered in some detail. The account of the raising of Jairus' daughter is to be found in Matthew 9:18-19, 23-26; Mark 5:21-24, 35-43; and again in Luke 8:40-42, 49-56. It is within Mark that we find the first and most comprehensive account, so it is to him that we turn for most of our information.

JAIRUS' DAUGHTER

The first criticism of this story is the charge that the girl was not really dead. The ruler of the synagogue approached Jesus with the information that his daughter was at the point of death. Therefore, at the commencement of the story, as far as Mark informs us, the girl was not dead. It would seem unreasonable that Jairus would come seeking Jesus so that he could raise her from the dead. If this were true, then Jesus would have been accepted as merely one of the numerous magicians moving through the lands. It is easier to maintain that the girl was at the point of death and that Jairus wanted her restored from a critical illness. One has continually to remind himself that there was at this time no clear distinction between grave illness and death itself. Anyone who had become seriously ill was already under the spell of death and to recover would be to rob death. The use of the Greek word *life* here stands in direct contrast with *death* in other references Mark makes (12:27; 16:11). Though the girl was not yet dead, she was not living a life worthy of being called life.

Jesus responded to this request with the utmost urgency and moved quickly along to the house without hesitation. Here we see Jesus moving forward to an encounter with death, which was a challenge to his total ministry. He, too, had to take faith because the Father had entrusted him. To withdraw at this stage would have meant defeat for Jesus and victory for the

28

demonic, since this was the manner in which Jesus viewed the contest. On his way he met the woman with the issue of blood. This "adds veracity to the whole story, for there is no attempt to fit these stories together by any literary artifice, and by far the most acceptable explanation is that the events took place as they are reported."[10] No doubt the incident with the woman added to the tension of an already anxious father who had no time to waste. Then came the messengers' report that the daughter was dead. There was no reason for Jesus to continue his journey since the girl had died and there was seemingly nothing that he could do. But Jesus said to the father, "Do not fear, only believe" (Mark 5:36). Mark is very clever in that he does not give any opinion from Jesus, and thus we still do not know what Jesus' attitude actually was. "Mark uses a difficult expression: ὁ δὲ ᾿Ιησοῦς παρακούσας τὸν λόγον λαλούμενον. Παρακούσας [*Parakousas*] can mean either 'overhearing' or 'not heeding'. [Vincent] Taylor prefers the latter meaning; Jesus did not heed what was said by the messengers, which can mean . . . he did not believe that the child was dead, in spite of what they said. . . ."[11] For him it was not true, or if it was true, it did not stop him.

When Jesus entered the house of Jairus, the people were weeping and wailing loudly. Jesus said to them, "Why do you make a tumult and weep? The child is not dead but sleeping" (Mark 5:39). One cannot assume that Jesus did not think that the little girl was dead because all the evidence was against him. The mourners had gathered about and began to laugh at him, which showed their distrust of his statement. Perhaps they were friends and neighbors, who had watched and waited during the illness and then saw the girl lapse into death. Jesus was not going to tell them things that contradicted their own experiences. Perhaps they were professional mourners, who would never be called until death was certain. Their presence and their actions do indeed present a strong case that she had actually died.

In this context Jesus may have been expressing his view of death from the point of view of God, which would be an extension of the Old Testament concept. In death we sleep under

God's watchful care, and he will awaken the dead in his own time. "Man calls it death—but from the divine point of view it is a sleep—not the sleep of eternal inactivity, as when the idea of death as a sleep was first advanced, but a temporary state, by implication peaceful; from which there will be an awakening to a full existence with God. If this view goes a little beyond the evidence of the saying we are considering, it must be admitted that it accords more fully with all the facts."[12]

Whatever our personal reaction to the account may be, there is absolutely no doubt in the Gospels that the girl was actually dead since the Gospel writers relate this story to indicate Jesus' power over death. Though one might find that the other accounts vary and are not as straightforward in detail, he will nevertheless have to admit that this is precisely what Mark meant in the earliest account of this story.[13]

As one rereads this account, he is struck by the fact that so little is actually known about the girl. We do not know the nature of her illness, nor do we know anything about the length of her suffering. All these facts are laid aside to present her encounter with Jesus. What does come to our attention is the fact that Jesus worked simply out of compassion for the parents. Obviously, if the girl was dead she would suffer no more; therefore, raising her from the dead really could not have been done for her sake. It becomes apparent that the raising of this young girl was in fact done for the parents, who had suffered the great loss of their little daughter. Her illness and death gain significance only in the light of the grief of her parents.

Jesus moved forward in this situation with confidence and poise, looking intently at the seriousness of the matter without either belittling it or becoming anxious about it. He gave courage to the woman along the way as well as to the father, who must have been undergoing great personal agony. From these two vivid accounts of Jesus' encounters with death we see that he always faced up to the reality and the fact of death. He continually moves forward to meet it where it strikes. Certainly these two stories leave us with the most outstanding work of Christ which shows his uniqueness, and, even more, his outgoing compassion. The key to understanding the problem of death as shown by Jesus was through God's compassion toward man.

THE SON OF THE WIDOW OF NAIN

The other related story is the raising of the son of the widow of Nain (Luke 7:11-17). For some unknown reason this account appears only in the Gospel of Luke. The tendency of criticism at this point is to maintain that it must be fabrication. However, we cannot so easily dismiss this as such, for we have just seen the prototype in the Synoptic Gospels. Even though the facts are not given in the other Gospel accounts, the belief that Jesus had the power to raise the dead is confessed there. It may be that Mark was not present at the time and did not want to relate such an amazing story in the third person.

Some will continue to harp on the fact that the man was not really dead. The death in this story is far more tangible than that in the account of Jairus' daughter. The whole community was aware of the man's death; Jesus encountered the funeral march on the way to the burial grounds. It would be far easier to point a finger of scorn at the miracle than at the fact that the man was actually dead. When one has to deal with miracles, one miracle cannot really be considered more amazing than another; it is simply a matter of degree. The Gospel writers must have felt that they had in their own way told enough of the story to be convincing; it would have been impossible to relate the entire story. Just as in all the other Gospel writings, the authors were forced to pick and choose, perhaps not always using the best discretion. Also, it must be assumed that there were equally dramatic stories which did not enter the Gospels at all.

Of great interest to the reader is that in this account Luke uses for the first time ὁ Κύριος (the Lord), which implies that Jesus is Lord of life as well as Lord over death. He is Lord because he manifests a power beyond himself.

The death of the widow's son is even more tragic than that of Jairus' daughter. The widow of Nain, who had obviously lost her husband, had now lost her son—her only son—which meant that she would have to fend for herself. The entire community turned out to share in her sorrow because it too sensed the dire need of the widow as she stood alone in the world. A woman in the Near East with no male figure for support was completely alone and as good as dead.

Jesus again moved forward out of compassion for the bereaved rather than the deceased. The mourners were accepted as doing a necessary and proper function and consequently were not rebuked by Jesus. This indicates that there were acceptable means of grieving as well as the very objectionable wailings and tumults. Jesus seems to have stumbled on a particularly tragic death without being asked to the scene. He first gave comfort to the bereaved widow. His comfort did not come merely because of empathy but rather because he in fact could do something about the situation. Thus he said, "Do not weep." Contained within these words is the promise that something could and would be done because he did not rebuke the crowd for its mourning.

Then Jesus moved forward to the bier, and after some words and perhaps actions the man immediately sat up. Again there is absolutely no evidence of what Jesus might have said, other than the one recorded statement, or what in fact he did, leaving little room for the faith healer to conjure a ritual or formula. The words and actions apparently were so simple that they drew no attention to themselves. We are then simply told that he gave the son back to his mother. It is striking to note here also that nothing about the illness—its length or its nature— is known. There is also no indication of how long the son may have been dead.

Death in this story, as in the account of Jairus' daughter, is defeated not as much because it is evil as because Jesus wants to meet the needs of those left behind. Death seems to be a much different matter with Jesus confronting it, as somehow it mysteriously changes its fearful hold and perhaps even its very nature.[14]

He can recall the dead to return to life, as if, indeed, the fact of death is not so great an obstacle to God as it inevitably seems to man. Our Lord's action here is very much like that of arousing someone from sleep, although the idea of sleep is not mentioned in the passage. . . . It is perhaps worth noting that the natural tendency of a people with a long tradition of faith in God, is to think God is the cause of this remarkable event. [And it was easy for them to look beyond Jesus to God.] . . . It seems best to understand this miracle as our Lord's response to the tragic plight of the widow, and as an indication of his mastery over death—a mastery never idly displayed to the curious, but all the more real by being kept under control.[15]

Two other accounts must be examined for the sake of completeness, although they do not really fit in the same context. The first is about the healing of the epileptic boy who had fallen into a state in which he looked as if he were dead. But there is no indication that he was by any means dead (Mark 9:14-29). The second account is about the centurion's slave at Capernaum, in which he is described as "sick and at the point of death" (Luke 7:2). In this passage there is no indication that the slave had died. Thus, these accounts are ruled out because death is used only as a metaphorical term.

What, then, was Jesus' attitude toward his own death? This provocative question holds within it one of the great mysteries surrounding this entire study. There is perhaps no richer and more significant problem to be lifted up in the whole of the Gospel accounts. Our attitude toward death would be greatly enhanced and enlightened if we could come to some in-depth understanding of this question.

Whatever we may say of the marvel and the mystery, the sacrifice and the scandal, the aura and the atonement, in the last analysis we must reiterate that Jesus' death was a human death. This point cannot be stressed too emphatically because this is precisely what most of our theological reasoning fails to probe. The reality of his death is the one undeniable factor and as such it constitutes the most logical approach to the problem. It is for this human aspect that the creeds cried out. There is indeed much more that may be said in regard to its uniqueness,[16] its redemptive power, or even its cosmological significance, but first and foremost it was a human death.

The same point can be made with regard to the frequent assertion that Christ's death was not just physical death—it involved a spiritual "death" and desolation such as could only be experienced by the Incarnate Son of God. This may be fully granted, but it does not lessen the meaning of Christ's death as human death. Sometimes commentators refer to "mere physical death" as if it is really a matter of no account at all. This, at any rate, can be refuted from a consideration of the references in the gospels to Christ's death. Whatever deeper significance can rightly be ascribed to that death, it is also to be considered as a significant human death.[17]

If one denies the humanity of the death of Jesus, he perhaps overlooks God's purpose and plan contained within it and may indeed by his own reflections condemn it as stark foolishness. From a thorough reading of the New Testament, it would seem that the whole point of the Gospels is to build up to the *crescendo* of Christ's death, but to ignore or dismiss the human side will result in neither a complete nor a realistic theology. So it is to this objective fullness of Christ's death that we must now turn.

Jesus had begun his ministry with the full hope and expectation that the kingdom of heaven would come in due course, without the anticipation of his own personal death. It would be more than difficult for a man to venture out with the expectation that his mission and message would end in utter failure unless he had the power to see beyond his own time. Jesus must have been caught up in the early successes of his teaching and healing ministry. The acclamation that he received must have assured him that the kingdom had come upon the earth and had infused itself in the affairs of men. The Gospels tell us that the common people heard him gladly, so much so that they literally rushed from all over the countryside to listen or to be healed. Not all of those who came were shallow or superficial in their commitment to him; his word and deeds had spread to such an extent that he had become more than just a topic of discussion or a local spectacle.

Jesus fell quickly from his place of public esteem. The fall was so rapid that the Gospels do not even attempt to trace it or to analyze it. Death came to his mind "as the inexorable necessity," and it is from this awareness that he then began to turn to the thought that the kingdom is more futuristic.[18] Any attempt to make Jesus' death preplanned by God leads to Docetism and ultimately proceeds to the worship of a "robot" rather than a person. This does not mean, however, that the concept of the present kingdom was merely cast off, but rather that he set up the tension between the present and the future.

As Jesus became aware of his own impending death and its nature, he began to foretell it, as demonstrated in the Passion narratives of Mark 8:27-33; 9:30-32; and 10:32-34, which have their counterparts in the other Gospels. These statements began only after the confession of Peter at Caesarea Philippi, yet the actual thought came much earlier.[19] It is from the point of the confession that there appeared a new phase of Jesus' ministry. The call was for repentance as he moved toward Jerusalem. He turned from preaching to the multitudes to preaching to the intimate group of twelve. "His subject is not so much the kingdom as Himself, and in particular His death."[20]

One cannot evade Jesus' deliberate attempt to teach his disciples not only the fact of his death but also its nature. The message and the foretelling were bold and clear, and stemmed from a deep sense of dedication. He had to move to Jerusalem, where his death would be brought about by the leaders of the Jews. It would be preceded by physical punishment—mocking, spitting, and scourging. Jesus' death was not to be the end; it was to be followed by a resurrection.

There is no doubt in the Gospel accounts that Jesus must ($\delta\epsilon\hat{\iota}$) die. This imperative means two things to Denney. On the one hand, he views it as inevitable because the powers had risen to such a high fervor that they could not be turned back and hence they *must* ensnare Jesus. On the other hand, Denney maintains that Jesus must die in order to *fulfill* the mission he felt compelled to complete.

Jesus, we are told, came to see that His death was inevitable because of the forces arrayed against Him; but being unable, as the well-beloved Son of the Father, merely to submit to the inevitable or to encounter death as a blind fate, He reconciled Himself to it by interpreting it as indispensable, as something which properly entered into His work and contributed to its success. It became not a thing to endure, but a thing to do. The passion was converted into the sublimest of actions.[21]

The death of Jesus was brought about by the conspiracy of the Jewish leaders who looked upon him as an out-and-out foe. No one can attempt to answer the question of why Jesus had to die in this manner. It is all a part of the greater problem of evil. Basically one can only point to the evil inherent in man. Although Jesus' death was a common one which other innocent men had suffered, yet it was maliciously plotted that he should be killed for political gain.

His death was planned by the Jewish leaders who tried to take him by subtlety and kill him (Mk. 14:1); the betrayal by one of the twelve was an important factor in the events which led to his arrest (Mk. 14:44f); once he was arrested, the leaders of the Jews provided false witnesses to condemn him, and in spite of the judicial decision of Pilate, that Jesus was innocent, he was delivered up to be crucified. . . . The gospels do not present these distasteful facts in order to elicit our pity for the victim, nor our condemnation of his enemies. The emphasis is upon the stark facts—facts, we must remember, in their outward appearance, not uncommon in those times. Indeed, looked at from the point of view of a Roman these events would probably be regarded as sordid and boring; the sort of thing that did happen from time to time in those remote corners of the empire. Again, we insist that this is certainly not all there is to be considered in the death of Christ—all subsequent Christian history shows that to be false—but in its simplest outline here is a man facing death. Whatever else it is, it is brutal, sordid, painful human death; not the worst kind of death anyone could face, but bad enough to be considered one of the most brutal and unjustified, even on the grounds of common decency and justice.[22]

Jesus' death was one of a common criminal by means of crucifixion outside the city walls of Jerusalem. And how did he look upon his own death? From what has been said previously, a strong case could be made that Jesus knew not only that he would die but also *how*. Perhaps one who was purported to have had a dramatic birth, and a unique life, could expect only an extraordinary death. There seems always to have been the freedom to turn away from the grim future just ahead. To what intent and purpose Jesus felt that he was responding to God's plan for him can never be discerned.

Jesus drew away to the seclusion of the Garden of Gethsemane with James, John, and Peter. It was to this intimate group that Jesus was able to express even more of his nature and purpose.

"My soul is very sorrowful even to death; remain here and watch" (Mk. 14:34); cf. Matthew 26:38, which adds "with me" to the Marcan form. The first part of this saying is an echo, rather than a quotation, apparently based on Psalms 42:5 and 43:5. "Why are you cast down, O my soul?" These two Psalms both deal with the disquietude, or in modern terminology, "depression" of a man who normally enjoys fellowship with God. In the first instance the depression is caused by a loss of the sense of God's presence. "My soul thirsts for God, for the living God." "When shall I come and behold the face of God?" (Ps. 42:2). This desolation is increased by the jibes of those who continually say unto him: "Where is your God?" In the second instance, it is more plainly stated that it is a man's enemies which cause him "to go mourning". In both cases the solution to the difficulty is the same. "Hope in God; for I shall again praise him, my help and my God."[23]

Here Jesus turned to the depth of the thought of the psalmists to express not only his discouragement but also his trust in God, the failures that pitted man against hope in God.

The other aspect of this saying is the thought of "even unto death." This idea finds its background in the Old Testament as well as in the Apocrypha. It comes most specifically from the passage in the Book of Jonah which tells that Jonah was made weak from the wind and the sun; and wishing to escape, he said, "It is better for me to die than to live" (4:8). From what has already been discussed, one realizes that Jesus' words did not come from the knowledge of the weight of his own death, though he knew something of it. Rather, it was only at this point that he began to realize fully the magnitude of his task. We cannot avoid the fact, however much we want, that Jesus was afraid of death. This is a difficult position for most Christians to accept because they cannot see Jesus as one afraid of death or anything else. The general assumption is made that the Christian ought not to fear death because Christ showed no fear of death. We could not be farther from the truth. This belief has no doubt caused a great amount of undue anguish and suffering for the committed Christian, who finds that there is much to fear in the unknown realm of death and is criticized, either by society or mostly by his conscience, because he is thought to be showing a weakness in his beliefs. One cannot, regardless of his personal beliefs, come to death without some serious apprehensions if he is of sound mind. However, we are not in the least moved to assign these same feelings to Jesus. Accepting Jesus as a man is indeed hardest at this point.

Professor Oscar Cullmann tells that he has received more criticism of his small book entitled *Immortality of the Soul or Resurrection of the Dead?* than any other of his writings. But of all the bitter criticism he received he could say, "So far, no critic of either kind has attempted to refute me by exegesis, that being the basis of our study."[24] He does a remarkable job of comparing and contrasting the death of Socrates as revealed in *Phaedo* and that of Jesus as revealed in the New Testament.

The Synoptic Evangelists furnish us, by and large, with a unanimous report. Jesus begins "to tremble and be distressed", writes Mark (14:33). "My soul is troubled, even to death", He says to His disciples. Jesus is so thoroughly human that He shares the natural fear of death. Jesus is afraid, though not as a coward would be of the men who will kill Him, still less of the pain and grief which precede death. He is afraid in the face of death itself. Death for Him is not something divine: it is something dreadful. Jesus does not want to be alone in this moment. He knows, of course, that the Father stands by to help Him. He looks to Him in this decisive moment as He has done throughout his life. He turns to Him with all His human fear of this great enemy, death. He is afraid of death.[25]

In contrast, Socrates was calm and unassuming as he approached death and immortality by lifting the hemlock. He died rather nonchalantly. Jesus was depressed, anxious, in a state of agony, and in need of the companionship of his disciples. On the cross he uttered the cry of desperation: "My God, my God, why hast thou forsaken me?"

One's attention is certainly drawn to the parallels that Professor Cullmann makes, but one is even more conscious of the dissimilar factors. Jesus was under commitment; vocationally he was integrally tied to the will of God; and hence he was directly responsible to God. A great part of his tension came from his desire to do what was right and yet never quite knowing what was right. Socrates was responsible to no one and thus could and did act as a free agent. Death came to Socrates at the end of life, but for Jesus it was only the start of life which had entry into deeper dimensions. Jesus was calling forth his disciples to life commitment while Socrates as a teacher knew that his thoughts, if truth, would continue whether they were adhered to or not. Jesus was wrestling with cosmic dimensions while Socrates was proving his philosophy and making the best of an unforeseen situation. The entire nature of death was different—Socrates died an honorable death whereas Jesus died the most contemptible death, the death of a criminal upon the cross. And of course the difference in sheer physical pain was enormous.

Basically Jesus' whole attitude toward death and that of Socrates were radically different in that Socrates viewed it as freedom from an imprisoned life whereas Jesus saw it as man's only imprisonment. All these points should be lifted up, but what Professor Cullmann says is most important and ought to resound again and again—Jesus was afraid of death. This is self-evident, and since his death has been accepted as unique, no comparison need be cited except as a matter of interest. Cullmann calls us sharply back to the humanity of Jesus. Whatever else may be said, Jesus died a human death and had human fears concerning it. His fear of death was due more to the tremendous burden of responsibility upon him than to the ponderous unknown, which accounts for his trembling. Death was the greatest terror that could face Jesus, for death means that one is under the powers of the demonic and thus farthermost from God.

Because it is God's enemy, it separates us from God, who is Life and the Creator of all life. Jesus, who is so closely tied to God, tied as no other man has ever been, for precisely this reason must experience death much more terribly than any other man. To be in the hands of the great enemy of God means to be forsaken by God. In a way quite different from others, Jesus must suffer this abandonment, this separation from God, the only condition really to be feared. Therefore He cries to God: "Why hast thou forsaken me?" He is now actually in the hands of God's great enemy.

We must be grateful to the Evangelists for having glossed over nothing at this point. Later (as early as the beginning of the second century, and probably even earlier) there were people who took offence at this—people of Greek provenance. In early Christian history we call them Gnostics.[26]

Perhaps the most striking factor in all the Gospel accounts dealing with the death of Christ is that the emphasis always is one of physical death. In Jerusalem, Jesus was led to a very common and excruciating death. There is here no theological implication: it is presented as a story of a man who was to die by being crucified. The theology of the event certainly came afterward; this plainly was a physical death from which he sought escape. First and foremost the Gospels give us an account of a real death faced in a realistic manner. This is the basic thought we learn from the New Testament concerning death.

Jesus had proclaimed to his disciples, "Do not fear those who kill the body but cannot kill the soul; rather fear him who can destroy both soul and body in hell" (Matt. 10:28; see also Luke 12:4-5). There is a world of difference between a fear of men who can bring about your death and a fear of death itself, the first being an earthly fear and the second the ultimate fear of being under the spell of death. Jesus was afraid and rightly so, but not ultimately afraid. Beyond this fear was the light of confidence that this same God, the God he served, would somehow see him through.

The fear rested more in his own confidence: "Will I be able to undergo this task and see my way through? Can I remain faithful under such a burden?" He was like a warrior doing battle without knowledge of the enemy's power—more colossal than a David fighting a Goliath of evil. Always there was the risk or uncertainty that he might go down to defeat. It would have been no struggle at all if the score was already known by Jesus. There was also the hope that he would fill the expectations of God and the needs of those he would have to confront for generations unborn. This was no battle fought off in the hazy realms of Sheol but rather the turning point of the cosmos.

Because Jesus underwent death in all its horror, not only in His body, but also in His soul ("My God, why hast thou forsaken me"), and as He is regarded by the first Christians as the Mediator of salvation, He must indeed be the very one who in His death conquers death itself. He cannot obtain this victory by simply living on as an immortal soul, thus fundamentally *not* dying. He can conquer death only by actually dying, by betaking Himself to the sphere of death, the destroyer of life, to the sphere of "nothingness", of abandonment by God. When one wishes to overcome someone else, one must enter his territory. Whoever wants to conquer death must die; he must really cease to live—not simply live on as an immortal soul, but die in body and soul, lose life itself, the most precious good which God has given us. For this reason the Evangelists, who none the less intended to present Jesus as the Son of God, have not tried to soften the terribleness of His thoroughly human death.[27]

With these thoughts as background for his death, is it any wonder that he was shaken to the point of being afraid? And in a real sense followers too have the right to shrink back from death. Anything other than this is to ascribe to Jesus something less than full humanity. Regardless of what effects this may have on one's personal faith, these are the facts and this is what the Evangelists wanted others to see. This by no means should weaken one's faith but rather increase it, because Jesus faced up to the realities of death and, for the first time in history, here was a man who *did* something about death. There was no attempt to deny or belittle it as other religions of the world would have us do. But the story does not end here, and it is not right that one should have a fixation on Jesus' death or its agony, as a whole host of Christian people believe. It is a victory through fear and trembling, hence all the more a victory. Jesus refused the sympathetic narcotic so that he would be fully conscious of death and its meaning. The narcotic would only have allowed Jesus a further opportunity to escape the stark reality of death. This was not a man seeking the easy way out. The Gospels drive one to look beyond the crucifixion. In fact, they tell about the death of their leader with undue constraint. Their story is briefly told without adding philosophy, emotion, condemnation, or sentimentality.

It is very evident that there is a great gap in contemporary writing with regard to the "last things," especially about the meaning of death. But whatever disappointments the original disciples must have felt over the humiliation and subsequently the crucifixion, which was followed by the shock and the embarrassment of it all, they nevertheless overcame them. They were so changed that "the centre of gravity in their world changed, and their whole being swung round into equilibrium in a new position. Their inspiration came from what had once alarmed, grieved, and discomfited them. The word they preached was the very thing which had once made them afraid to speak."[28] They must have somehow been convinced that their Master, who had died, had survived death. This sent them seeking an answer to what was in fact a gross contradiction of their concept of the messiahship. "Closer scrutiny of the New Testament writings themselves soon suggests that the origins of Christian soteriology constitute a problem far more complex than Christian *apologia* is accustomed to admit."[29] The members of the early church were certainly perplexed by the entire problem of soteriology, but even so they were willing to work on it and develop it rather than hide it as many in the twentieth century wish to do.

It is evident from sources that "the Christian Church has never agreed to be silent as to the fate of the lost; the majority of its representatives have asserted the doctrine of Eternal Evil with vigor and decision. The idea that we should have nothing to say about the final fortunes of humanity is a recent discovery, and is due to the pressure of sustained criticism, both within and without the Church."[30]

The failure to develop a theology of eschatology has made a

large gap in an otherwise well-defended facade. It could be likened to a garrison; or to the Nazi Western Wall, which was rendered useless because of some exposure such as an open door or roof. Theologians continue to build and rebuild the walls, which is of little avail with such a vulnerable and unprotected gap. Is it not a matter of making the strongest point the weakest by a complete inversion of the theological system? Dare we hope that the critics of the faith will desist from attacking the lines of least resistance? It is precisely eschatology on which most of the scorn and abuse are poured. The failure to defend man's destiny in Christianity is already to admit defeat. One dare not neglect a faith firmly rooted in its eschatology.

The "last things" cannot be put down (nor will they be), for resurrection must be consistent with truth. To deny any aspect of the wholeness of Christianity is to deny Christianity. However insecure we may personally feel about the "last things," the problems still confront the whole church and must be grappled with so that one may see theologically how all the pieces fit. An attempt will be made here.

There is a frightening passage in the Gospel of Matthew (26:24) that is reported as a part of the words of Jesus. In it Jesus issued a condemnation of Judas by saying that it would have been better if he had not been born. It is a saying that one attempts to rule out because it seems inconsistent with the other sayings of Jesus. It is, however, idiomatic and perhaps as such was rather popular. The origins are at least as old as 2 Enoch (38:2). It seems that this is no doubt the meaning Jesus had in mind, and consequently it is not as drastic as it may first appear.

No statement of Jesus has caused greater distress and mental anguish than his statement that the sin of blasphemy against the Holy Spirit will never be forgiven. The exact implications will always remain obscure. But viewed within the context, it is a comment to the scribes who had acknowledged the works of Jesus to be the work of the demons.

In so doing they blasphemed against that divine spirit of compassion which inspired the healing ministry of the Saviour. They sinned against love; and this was ever the kind of offence that was most hateful to Jesus. Hence He declared with passionate indignation that their attitude was beyond the reach of forgiveness. This pronouncement of His cannot, however, be said to convey a sentence of personal and irrevocable doom unless we can be sure that it was directed against individual men. And we cannot attain to such certainty. Rather does it seem that the offence of the Scribes was committed by them as a class or party, not as separate persons. This interpretation is rendered probable by the fact that the Jewish mind was accustomed to the idea that nations and bodies of men could commit an unforgiveable sin. Thus it is said in the *Book of Jubilees* that when the children of Israel break the law of circumcision, "there will be no more pardon or forgiveness unto them for all the sin of this eternal error." (Jub. 15:34).[31]

If Jesus hurled this condemnation at one specific person, it would be a blatant contradiction of all one can gather concerning him from the New Testament. It would be hard to believe that man could reap eternal condemnation for one action. But even sharper is the realization that Paul was a zealous member of the Pharisees, the group Jesus had in mind when he spoke. Paul would have stood under this condemnation, yet he was the same man who was so forgiven for "his sin against the Holy Spirit" that he became a leader of the church. As a case in point, one may have to withdraw from the idea that this concerned an individual and conclude that it meant the whole body of Pharisees.

In the Gospel account it is clear that good and evil are opposed to each other as light is to darkness, with each having its own goal. However, when one considers the word *destruction,* its meaning remains unclear.

Indeed, the habit of applying the methods of minute verbal analysis to such words of Jesus is unhistorical in spirit, and is not conducive either to reverence or understanding. It distracts attention from the religious and prophetic force of the evangelic sayings, and directs the mind to the mere details of their expression. It thus subordinates that which is vital, and that of which we can be sure, to formal peculiarities which are usually doubtful and always of minor moment. Also, it compels us to bring the utterances of our Lord into the region of laboured controversy; and whatever is made the subject of prolonged debate begins to wear an aspect of uncertainty. The longer one studies the works of partisan divines the more one is convinced that the path of wisdom lies in refusing to base doctrinal conclusions on any single text or on any merely verbal grounds. No doctrine is secure that is not supported by a persistent element in the Gospel records.[32]

There is, however, running through the entire Gospel, the idea of exclusion. The theme occurs too frequently and in too many separate places to deny it a position of authenticity. The King is seen as closing the gates and excluding those who remain outside. He keeps the gates shut even to those who continue to wail outside the walls (Matt. 25:41-46). This comes as a serious and stern warning from the Lord, uttered with concern and compassion.

It belongs to a minor strain which is heard in the voice of our Lord—a sadness of foreboding, a stern perception of ominous possibilities. There is a broad and easy way that leads to destruction; it profits a man nothing if he gain the whole world and lose his own life; it had been well for Judas if he had never been born; apostate disciples are as salt that has lost its virtue and is henceforth good for nothing but to be cast out and trodden under foot of men; there is an obscurity of the soul, wherein the very light is as darkness; there are those whose lives are like painted tombs full of dead men's bones and all uncleanness; there are offenders for whom it were better that a millstone were hanged about the neck and they were drowned in the depth of the sea. These are all sayings that are weighted with a burden of prophetic warning. They compel us to recognize, with an awe of spirit which is the deeper the more humbly we acknowledge the authority of Jesus, that He believed in an immeasurable danger which threatened the souls of men; a horror of great darkness from which they had to be delivered; a desert of dreary exile towards which the beloved race of mortals was straying with careless feet.[33]

The other aspect of the Lord's teachings is more hopeful. If one understands the concept of Gehenna, as the common belief as a rather fixed state regarding the theory of destiny, one finds the tradition does not leave sufficient material to assume that the fate of the lost is in any way different from that of those revealed in Jesus' apocalyptic prophecies. One cannot enlarge on these concepts of doom, amplifying them all out of proportion, for one must realize that there is an element of teaching here. It seems ironic, but the tendency of the far extremes on both sides of the Christian continuum has been to lift out one phrase and expound it for use directly against the opposing side. Yet, they are both guilty of the same mistake.

The call of Jesus in the account of Luke 12:58-59 is a call to place our affairs in order before the coming of the Lord. In this passage there is no information concerning the duration of the penalty.

We may conjecture, indeed, that if He had really declared any definite doctrine on this subject we would not have had to seek for it in the obscure corners of the Gospel story, in the details of a picture, in the chance turning of a phrase.

Jesus certainly taught that there would be degrees of future punishment and a greater and lesser condemnation. . . . In short, the three earlier Evangelists do ascribe sayings to Jesus which tend to modify the accepted doctrine of perdition, though they do not afford a basis for confident conclusions.[34]

Jesus was placed in a precarious position by being forced to take a stand either with or against the Sadducees (Mark 12:18-27). The question was certainly one which had no easy way out; it was designed specifically to ensnare him. No doubt the rabbis had pondered over it for some time. Within this passage is the controversy of the various opinions concerning man's destiny in the departed realms. The Sadducees are revealed as those who say that there is no resurrection (ἀνάστασιν). By word of condemnation in Acts 23:8 the Sadducees are said to deny the resurrection, angels, and the spirit (πνεῦμα). The Pharisees believed in these things, and it became a matter which pitted the Sadducees against the Pharisees, leaving an irreparable cleavage.

The concept of the resurrection of the dead was widespread, as shown in Mark 12:25 (ὅταν . . . ἐκ νεκρῶν ἀναστῶσιν), which appears elsewhere in the New Testament and is certainly consistent with Hebrew thought. The Hebrews believed man to be a psychophysical organism; there could be no afterlife without the body, even though it was a spiritual body. Without the reconstitution of both body and soul it could not really be considered an existence. Resurrection is viewed as the predestinated experience of all Jewish people, which does not take into consideration any ethical qualifications. The passage goes on to say that the resurrection is inevitable because it was ordained by God; hence the patriarchs are not dead but living.

Jesus sided with the Pharisees in this debate in the communal as well as the individualistic sense. He believed that the righteous dead would enter Sheol but would rise again to partake in the kingdom of God (Matt. 22:23-33). The Sadducees' argument proceeded along the lines of Mosaic Law because to them this was the only proper means of argument. Although their contention seems absurd from our point of view, this was their formula. It is very possible that this was an old argument that had been used successfully to confound believers of the resurrection, as well it might have. There is absolutely no ground to maintain that this was a new problem for them. The concept of levirate marriage was developed fully almost to obscure the issue. Jesus' reply began by stating that their presuppositions were wrong. One cannot assume that the future kingdom will be just an extension of the existing life, and this is where they err. Rather, there are new dimensions and ramifications far beyond their imagination, and the dead are like the "angels." This existence is beyond the present life and obviously of a higher order. Jesus sustained the thought that men will continue with bodies which are transformed and glorified as are the angels'.[35]

In conclusion he challenged the accusers because they did not know the power of God. In a real sense he succeeded in returning the question to the Sadducees in what was a most offensive retort. Jesus picked up the discussion, arguing from their authority, that of the Scriptures; he pointed out that it was the Sadducees who continually harped on the fact that their God was indeed the God of Abraham, Isaac, and Jacob.

The implication was that their God must be one who cares for these men or else God is somehow greatly diminished. He is then not the great, awesome God who called everything into being.

If God had been merely the nation's God, then the immortality of the nation would be all we could properly hope for. But if God is the God of individuals, if individuals can enter into fellowship with Him, if individuals are precious in His sight, then our hope in God necessarily becomes a hope for the individual.

The argument is unanswerable; and is indeed the only unanswerable argument for immortality that has ever been given, or ever can be given. It cannot be evaded except by a denial of the premises. If the individual can commune with God, then he must matter to God; and if he matters to God, he must share God's eternity. For if God really rules, He cannot be conceived as scrapping what is precious in His sight. It is in the conjunction with God that the promise of eternal life resides.[36]

This comes from the logical extension of a personalized religion developed to its fullest.

Jesus' argument here rested on the existing beliefs, and he made no attempt to reform these thoughts. He merely pointed out the glaring inconsistency in what they upheld, on the one hand, and, on the other hand, what they in fact believed. There was no more shattering attack which could have been leveled at these devout Jews than an approach to the Torah.

The call to life is more than a return to the shadowy existence of death. This at best is a feeble existence placed beyond the realm of God—not past his awareness but beyond his power. However, Jesus tells us that there is more than this, for there is complete communion with God. A resurrection of the whole of man is needed before this participation can be complete. Luke has a variant on the theme (20:38); in this book Jesus makes the statement that "all live to him [God]." He teaches that all men regardless of their moral status live in the future life to God. The just and the unjust, the good and the evil, and the moral and the immoral shall be brought into the resurrection. This, of course, runs counter to the arguments proposed by both Matthew and Mark.

The New Testament stands out against its background and other writings of the period because the concept of resurrection takes a far more prominent position. The resurrection of Jesus becomes the core of the Gospel account, and the entire ministry and teaching of Christ are seen through it or are reflected by it. The resurrection is stamped on every page of the New Testament, which in turn transforms all former Hebrew ideas and concepts. However, when one comes to a close scrutiny of the nature and the meaning of the resurrection from the sources of the New Testament, there is no clear picture. Rather, one finds various fragments which, when fitted together, do not make a logical or consistent whole.

While the criticism comes because of a lack of unity, there is absolutely no question about the *fact* of the resurrection. This above all else stands out. It was this experience that transformed the unmentionable into the very core of the disciples' proclamation. Whatever had been the disheartening effects of the crucifixion, the first disciples became convinced beyond a reasonable shadow of doubt that their Master rose again from the dead. It was from this assurance that they moved forward with such force and vigor, cutting—then and now—a deep pattern into the fabric of the lives of men.

The attention of the New Testament is directed to the marvel and the mystery of the Life it offers. Perhaps not to distract from this glory, the state of the unrighteous is seldom mentioned. The disciples' concern was for those who would be a part of the "new creation." They hardly addressed themselves to the state of the unrighteous but rather maintained that they also must be present as individuals, whole and conscious "on that day." So filled were they with the glory of this experience that they did not want their sight tarnished by the unregenerate.

The concept of a literal physical resurrection is not to be attributed to the New Testament. In resurrection individuals are to be embodied; thus, they could never be confused with the free-floating spirits of the Greeks. Any statement in regard to the new body must be sheer conjecture. However, one can conclude that resurrection will involve the full human nature of the individual. There will be no need to continue sex relationships since there will be no further need for sex (Mark 12: 24-25; Matt. 22:29-30; Luke 20:34-35). Obviously it is maintained that procreation is a part of the temporal order and therefore is not needed for the fulfillment of life. Jesus also made reference to eating and drinking in the kingdom (Luke 22:18, 30; Mark 14:25; Matt. 26:29). Scholars maintain that these terms are figurative and these activities are not really a part of the kingdom, for we are "like angels." The assumption is that angels do not eat. The argument should be based on the nature of these bodies. If they are to be living physical organisms, then they will require nourishment; but if they transcend physical existence, there cannot be any form of nourishment as we know it, nor can sex persist.

The core of Matthew and that of Mark (Matt. 22:30; Mark 12:25-27) make it plain that there is not to be a general resurrection but rather one of the righteous. A case can also be made that the earlier texts of the Lukan account taught only a resurrection of the righteous.

In the Hebrew mind a general resurrection was not a prerequisite for a general judgment. There could be, according to earlier apocalyptic thought, a final judgment without a bodily form. Such an illustration can be found in the Book of Jubilees (23:31). In Ethiopic Enoch 91-101 there is likewise a final judgment to which only the spirits of the righteous are raised. The Jews took in universal judgment along with universal resurrection, the logical counterpart, but they do not necessarily go together.

The New Testament makes no attempt to prove the fact of Christ's resurrection from the point of the belief in a general resurrection which was so widely claimed at that time. Rather, these writers' whole argument hinges on the resurrection of Christ and moves on from this. It would be wrong to assume that this was their only ground for hope, as many accepted the common belief from the Pharisees or on the grounds of Platonic discussions. The Hasidim had proved it with their lives, and it followed that this was the extension of God's love. So the resurrection of Christ became a case in point of the already accepted views.

By his resurrection, Jesus further proved the argument that the Hebrew God was a god of the living, not a god of the dead. He was not only the God of Abraham, Isaac, and Jacob but also the God of Jesus Christ, for he had drawn all these men to himself.

Men who had found it not altogether impossible to continue thinking (as their fathers had done) of Abraham, Isaac and Jacob as being long ago dead and done with. . . . That the patriarchs were dear to God and must accordingly share in His eternity is a thought that arrests; but that Jesus Christ was dear to God and must share in His eternity is a thought that compels. And again, that the children of Israel are so one with the patriarchs that they too must be immortal is a thought that arrests; but that the saints are so one with Christ that they too must be immortal is a thought that compels.[37]

Running throughout the religious beliefs of the ancient Near East was the concept of judgment. Israel was no exception. These beliefs were brought into the New Testament, and consequently Christianity included a doctrine of judgment.

One of the basic discussions is raised in the parable of the rich man and Lazarus (Luke 16:19-31), which conveys the typical Jewish imagery down to our day. It proceeds on the grounds that the ultimate fate of the individual is determined immediately after death. As to the test or qualifications for entry into either portion of the future, no norm or standard is laid down. The rich man does not measure up to the standards given by "Moses and the prophets," while at the same time Lazarus is rewarded for his observance of them. This stands in agreement with Jesus' statement to the thief on the cross (Luke 23:43).

It is disappointing to realize that the story of Lazarus is the only insight we have from Jesus concerning the conditions of life in Hades. It is seen that souls are segregated with regard to righteousness or evilness. There is, moreover, the ability to conceive or visualize life in the other area. Here also is the beginning of reward and punishment, but one is uncertain whether this is the intermediate state or the final state. One can conclude that Jesus certainly believed that departed spirits continued to exist and that they were cognizant of one another. But in any case there is a separation greater than one is able to communicate.

Although the fire in the parable may be symbolic and is similar to that in the religion of the Semites, it cannot be neglected, for it conveys something dangerous which ought to be avoided at any cost. It is a stern warning and as such one dare not ignore it. However, it is equally wrong to dwell on the torment or cleansing aspects because they simply are not there. This probably stems from a familiar parable since specific names are used. Jesus did not tamper with the details of the story. He placed the emphasis on what a grievous error it is to pass by one who is in need. To do so will be catastrophic.

The word *Hades* appears four times in the Gospels. "In Matt. 11:23 (= Lk. 10:15) Jesus declares that Capernaum shall go down to Hades. Concerning His church that is to be built upon the rock, He affirms that 'the gates of Hades shall not prevail against it' (Mt. 16:18). The other reference is in the story of Dives and Lazarus, where it is said that after the death and burial of the rich man, 'in Hades he lifted up his eyes, being in torments, and seeth Abraham afar off, and Lazarus in his bosom' (Lk. 16:23)."[38] The story of the rich man and Lazarus relates Hades to the concept of torment. Here the traditional idea of the underworld is presented with its apocalyptic imagery. Either Jesus used these same familiar thought patterns or they were attributed to him. The coming of the Parousia diminished any strong interest in the belief in Hades.

No intelligent Jewish believer thought of Hades as a state in which the righteous dead experienced anything else than pure happiness—a happiness only slightly less than the full glory of the Kingdom. And this was probably the character of the primitive Christian hope.

It is true that the doctrine of Hades does not hold any prominent place in the New Testament. . . . The Intermediate State, therefore, held a small place in their thoughts, being cast into shadow by the expectation of the Second Advent, the great Reckoning, and the end of the world.[39]

The concept of Gehenna has come here at the last. Although the word *Gehenna* appears only twelve times in the New Testament, there are several other terms used for the concept. In the Synoptic Gospels the words are reported to be Christ's own. Other terms used are "the furnace of fire, where men will weep and gnash their teeth" (Matt. 13:42), "eternal fire" or "unquenchable fire" (Matt. 18:8; 25:41; Mark 9:43, 48), and "eternal punishment" (Matt. 25:46). As has been shown previously, the concept of Gehenna was very fluid and varied even among rabbis of the same period. Dr. Edward Langton analyzes the various concepts of Gehenna, but it will suit our purposes best to look at his summary:

The passages which have been indicated show quite clearly that the conception of Gehenna was a fluid one during the centuries immediately preceding the time of Jesus. Now one shade of meaning appears, now another. When therefore our Lord speaks of the consignment of the wicked to "Gehenna" or to "everlasting" or "eternal" fire, the historical context alone does not enable us to define the precise meaning of His words. From such criteria as the literature of the period offers alone we cannot say whether for Jesus Gehenna was a place of intermediate punishment or of final doom. . . . It behoves us therefore to exercise the utmost caution in dealing with a subject which throughout the period of revelation was treated with so much reserve. From the general nature of our Lord's teaching we may safely conclude that He conceived of the punishment of the wicked in Gehenna as a spiritual punishment.[40]

Summary

In the New Testament there is no attempt on the part of Jesus to deny or belittle the nature or the fact of death. Jesus always moved forward to meet and defeat evil, and this action culminated in the raising of Jairus' daughter and the son of the widow of Nain. There was no hesitation as Jesus calmly and assuredly went out to confront, to challenge, and to change death and its very nature. He demonstrated that he not only is Lord of Life but also has power over death, man's last enemy. Because Jesus faced death calmly and realistically, one can view his own death in this manner with the knowledge that Jesus has changed death.

Death is looked upon as a fact and a grim reality which must be confronted without evasion or suppression. This came from the "naturalness" and the closeness of death in the life of the Hebrews. They believed in their earliest thoughts that only death could separate man from God. With the rise of the Hasidim came the belief that if God was God at all, his people would never be separated from him. Out of this tradition came the Pharisees, who held to a physical resurrection. Jesus took up their argument with his testimony and miracles of resurrection. He pointed out that God is not just a God of Israel but of individuals, who are precious in his sight, and thus the hope of the resurrection is for the individual.

Jesus' first concern in encountering death was compassion for the bereaved family. His request that they end their mourning came not from some glib optimism but rather because, as his statements implied, he could do something about death. He did not attempt to maintain that death was to come to an end, for it still held its sway, but ultimately it was defeated by the God of the Living through his power. Jesus invoked the people to end their fears and continue to believe in God. It becomes apparent that the raising of these two people was in fact done for their parents, who had suffered such great losses. All other details of their illnesses are suppressed to show Jesus' confrontation and compassion. Throughout these incidents we seem to detect an air of quiet confidence and understanding sympathy emanating from Jesus. He acted out of compassion for the bereaved rather than for the deceased.

There is througout the life and teachings of Jesus the concept that he *must* die in order to fulfill his mission and purpose. The death that Jesus faced was an excruciating physical death which many common criminals faced. The New Testament strongly asserts that he died a real death. It was a death which Jesus feared because he, who had walked so close to God, would now come into the hands of the demonic and it was this separation that was so terrifying. Death for Jesus was the consummation of his life, and it was only through his death that he could offer man any hope for the future. He defeated death through his own death and hence changed its nature and power. His death became the center of his preaching and eventually the center of preaching for the entire church.

There are many remnants in New Testament eschatology that are carry-overs of earlier forms of religion. Jesus did not attempt to change the outmoded forms but accepted them as they were presented. His work was to develop the essence of religion without necessarily destroying the form. Thus, one cannot determine whether Jesus saw beyond these archaic forms. There is no word from him which stabilizes the concepts of heaven and hell, and the way is open to see these as spiritual states. Most of the rigidity of Christian eschatology comes from isolated passages and texts. One cannot assume that even Jesus could have lifted and changed all the incompatible irregularities and inharmonious elements in the Jewish religion. He was in basic agreement with the theology of the Old Testament, and essentially he did not attempt to change it.

It was the shock and the scandal of the death of their leader that truly embarrassed the members of the new community. However, his death began to take on new reality for them as both death and life became more vivid. The word the members of the New Testament community proclaimed was the "very thing which had once made them afraid to speak." Somehow they must have been convinced that their Master, who had died, had survived death. This sent them seeking an answer to what was in fact a gross contradiction of their concept of the messiahship. A closer scrutiny of the New Testament writings themselves soon suggests that the origins of the Christian apologia are more complex than we are accustomed to admit. The members of the early church were certainly perplexed by the entire problem of soteriology, but in spite of this they were willing to work on it and develop it rather than hide it. That which so embarrassed them now became the very core of their message and the seed of all Christian theology. So it has remained, and so it shall continue.

2

The Concept of Death in the Pauline Letters

The doctrine of the death of Christ and its significance was not Paul's theology, it was his gospel. It was all he had to preach.

—James Denney

AFTER examining the scant eschatology of the Old Testament and that of the Synoptic Gospels, one is both shocked and surprised to find that when he comes to Paul's writings, he has a massive mountain of material to examine. It is amusing to note that most critics maintain that Paul's eschatology cannot be separated from his theology, yet in practice they relegate this to the final chapter and in the last analysis rationalize their motives for doing so. Even this is quite unfair to the writings of Paul since it is an attempt to sift and sort his works in order to fit them into contemporary schemes of systematic theology. Scholars impose upon his writings thoughts and theologies that never once crossed his fertile mind.

For Paul eschatology was theology and theology was eschatology; the two were indivisible. There was no need to make these two fields into separate concepts, and consequently there was never any conscious attempt to develop their differences. Although it can easily be seen that both his theology and eschatology fluctuated during his lifetime, and even to unheard-of lengths after his death, Paul obviously saw no gross, glaring inconsistencies and no doubt would find himself uncomfortable in the modern framework of theological jargon.

Whereas we looked at a barren Synoptics, Paul calls us to an endless oasis of material in an otherwise desolate land. Previously it was necessary to seek with diligence in order to grasp and to study eschatology; now we are faced with such a flood of writings that only a very selective study can be made. One could not presuppose for a minute that Paul could have settled down to produce another Synoptic Gospel. This would have been quite wrong since he did not know Jesus as a youth and perhaps only briefly knew Jesus as a man. But on that Damascus road Paul met the Christ, the risen and ascended Lord, a meeting that put away all his previous notions and confronted him with such a dramatic challenge that he dared not refuse the "call." Thus, to approach the eschatology of Paul, we must be prepared to accept a completely different perspective. In order to gain a proper perspective, it is necessary to list several important factors which should be foremost in our minds when we pursue Paul's thought.

1. The theme of Paul's theology was inevitably the result of his encounter with the risen Christ. It was of no avail for him to wander about the empty tomb in hope that the Christ might return. Further, he could not dwell on the wonderful example or the marvelous teachings of Jesus because he simply had not been there. Any information as such had to be reconstructed from the disciples in the new churches, and therefore it was secondhand. But one cannot overlook the significance of the encounter with Christ. At once Paul's attitude toward the Christian community was changed. Much of his Judaism fell by the wayside and some had to be transformed, but the encounter formed the nucleus of his theology.

One should have no difficulty understanding why eschatology became the theme of Paul's theology, for it was the risen Lord who appeared to him. Henceforth Paul saw the "last things" first. Consequently we find in Paul the complete inversion of the Synoptic outlook.

One may further argue that this one instant was hardly

enough to do all that was needed for Paul's thought. In reply to this it could be said, first, that in this one fleeting moment Paul received all the assurance that Christians long for and thereafter he moved forward with the belief in the living God who entered into men's lives in the "here and now."

Second, Paul never attempted to rest on the laurels of this one encounter but rather pounded out his theology on the anvil of human experience, as James S. Stewart has stated. While this encounter was always *par excellence,* his whole life from this point on is presented as a dynamic, continuous encounter between God and himself. He could say, "Paul, an apostle of Christ Jesus." So Paul proclaimed the "last things" first, not so much because of their immanence but because of their importance in his life and indeed in the life of those to follow.

2. Paul spoke of the shadow of mortality which challenges and threatens everyone. Because he was threatened by death so many times in his own life, this to him was not some vague metaphor but rather one derived from personal experience. This can be discerned throughout his entire corpus in such statements as: "Why am I in peril every hour?" and "I die every day." After this he alluded to his personal difficulties: " . . . humanly speaking, I fought with beasts at Ephesus" (1 Cor. 15:30-32). Whatever else one might say about this passage or its context, it is certainly clear that Paul was in grave danger at Ephesus, for he was, as so often before, "near death" (2 Cor. 11:23). Was it precisely in circumstances such as this that Prisca and Aquila actually "risked their necks" for Paul's sake and for which he expressed his personal gratitude? (Rom. 16:3-4). This can never be answered with certainty.

It is quite evident that Paul did not draw attention to the dangers of his own life except as they appeared in relation to his correspondence. Again and again we see these fleeting references but are never led directly to the details; yet from all of this we can certainly surmise that Paul's life was in constant danger. In Asia he found himself, as it were, already under the sentence of death (2 Cor. 1:9). And again in the letter to the Philippians the possibility of death is mentioned (1:20).

Though there are numerous occasions such as these when he speaks of death, no doubt there were even more dangerous moments that have not come down to us. Perhaps by far the most common danger was that of being shipwrecked. This happened to Paul more than once (2 Cor. 11:25; Acts 27); his ship was also adrift for a night and a day (2 Cor. 11:25). Probably there were numerous occasions during his journeys when he was beset by all possible dangers (2 Cor. 11:26). At one time he just slipped through the hold of King Aretas (2 Cor. 11:32-33; Acts 9:23-25).

Thus, when Paul makes reference to death or dying, it is never superficial or affected; it comes from severe personal experience. Such statements as "Why am I in peril every hour?" (1 Cor. 15:30); "I die every day" (1 Cor. 15:31); "We are afflicted in every way" (2 Cor. 4:8); "always carrying in the body the death of Jesus" (2 Cor. 4:10); "while we live we are always being given up to death" (2 Cor. 4:11); "like men sentenced to death" (1 Cor. 4:9), are not merely metaphors. They have deep and poignant meaning. Paul believed he would have to encounter many "deaths" to follow Christ.

3. Paul drew a great deal of attention to himself as he stood in opposition to the Jerusalem church. He caused a great deal of tension within the church itself, which resulted in even further difficulties and rejections, to be discussed later at greater length. But one can discern that Paul was finally imprisoned in Rome, where he lived as a lonely old man distrusted by many of the churches. Forsaken and forgotten even by the church of Rome, he died the lonely and tragic death of a martyr, which was surpassed only by Christ's own. Certainly he bore the wounds of Christ in his body and died as he had lived, for Christ.

4. Paul's conversion to Christianity represents one of the most radical changes that anyone could undergo. His change from one of the most zealous opponents of the faith to the staunchest defender allowed him to run the whole gamut of psychological and spiritual change. Few people can be radically changed in the manner that Paul was. Because of this

cleavage, he did not see himself so much as a continuous being but rather as one who had two radically distinct lives. Consequently, he could speak of this in only the most severe and drastic terminology—as if he had "died." The distinction is never really clear in his reference to conversion because the words *life* and *death* are often used as metaphors. They are used as the only alternatives to express this profound and radical cleavage between the "old" man and the "new" man in Christ. Hence, Paul's figurative language became for him a reality.

5. The eschatology of the New Testament is essentially the eschatology of Paul; therefore, it is in the field of eschatology that Paul becomes the theologian *par excellence*. There are two reasons for this: first, he drowns out other competitors by sheer bulk; second, he devotes the whole of his writing to eschatology. So it is to Paul that the church must turn time and time again to find the Christian meaning of both life and death. In these matters he has become our authority and example.

With these concepts firmly fixed as a working reference for an understanding of Paul, one has more latitude to understand the technical aspects of Pauline eschatology. We should first turn our attention to Paul's authority and position in the early church. Although it would appear easy to adjudge this position from the now-existing sources, we come across some very interesting aspects that are conspicuous by their absence. The history of the early church is not so much one of marvel as it is one of mystery. For behind the exposition of the *more excellent way* there lay a seething cauldron of contempt, jealousy, and innuendo. No one was more at the base of these difficulties than Paul. Behind the Pauline corpus there was the hostile conflict between Paul and his opponents, who shall ever remain anonymous. The issues that the Gentile converts raised merely opened the door to answer far deeper and far more serious rifts. One of the first accusations hurled at Paul, this Jewish entrepreneur, concerned authority.

As Professor Henry Chadwick pointed out so skillfully in his Gifford Lectures at the University of St. Andrews in the 1962 series, Paul placed himself on a par with the other apostles. On the one hand, Paul maintained that he stood in direct line of the transmitted authority from Christ Jesus, which entitled him to a full and rightful apostleship. On the other hand, he claimed, because of his direct revelation of Christ, that he stood in a unique position, independent from all other apostles. It is not hard to see the difficulties to which this led, for one who had stood so far out of the church now claimed to be the Lord's specially appointed apostle and as such could act as a free agent quite independent of the others and in counter-distinction with the established church of Jerusalem. Since authority in the early church rested on that which one could witness to rather than that which one might possess in virtue or religiosity, Paul stood on solid ground and could not easily be shaken.

The problem of another gospel comes up in Galatians (1:6-8) and again at Corinth (2 Cor. 11:3-6). Also at Corinth the subject of a different Christ arose. This would lead to the conclusion that there were at least two divergent views concerning the gospels and the nature of the person of Jesus. The fact that Paul made no attempt to name names or parties would indicate that perhaps at this point they were so strong that he dared not attack them openly. Since he was in no position to challenge others in the church, he made only the most subtle attack.

"If they had been merely an irresponsible sect, Paul would surely have repudiated them with that vehement scorn of which he often shows himself so capable. Instead he refers to these opponents in an oblique way such as suggests embarrassment about their identity, especially since at the same time he shows the utmost consternation about their activity."[1] This was no doubt an attack on the nature of the teachings from the Jerusalem church, which would never have to answer for its authority. Anything less than this would not have been worthy of Paul's caution. So Paul was in disagreement with the very heart and core of all Christianity, the mother church at Jerusalem. He took his stand against the apostles, who had followed Jesus in his daily life and knew him so well, and the relatives of Jesus. This was no mean feat. He strongly proclaimed that he was correct and even the best traditions and deepest personal experiences were in error.

How could he for a moment believe that he, Paul, was right and the whole of the original church was in error? How could he, who saw Jesus perhaps only once, take a stand against those who dared to believe in Jesus from the very beginning? This is truly an interesting problem, but this is indeed what Paul did. The fact that he was able to win out in victory was wholly due to a chain of the most extraordinary events.

The most important event in this chain was, of course, the destruction of the early church, dispersing its members and—as far as one can discern—dispelling its writings, its history, and its traditions. Hence, with the earliest sources of the church destroyed and the dispersion of its members, there was the opportunity for new traditions and new leaders. Perhaps it is only because of this one historical event that eschatology today is what it is. Had it not been so, Paul may have become the first great leader of a schism within the ranks of Christianity. Because he did succeed and because of his latter-day high esteem throughout Christendom, the assumption has been that Paul was correct. But what of the Jerusalem theology? Might it not be far easier to assume that this is the better ground on which Christians should stand? Since Pauline theology is full and inclusive, it has become the theology of the Christian church and no doubt will continue uncontested.

The Jerusalem Christians must have viewed themselves as being continuous with the Jewish tradition and felt that there was no need for a radical break. They present Jesus as being pro-Jewish and confining his ministry to the Jews. This is brought home in the account of the Syrophoenician woman who sought out Jesus to save her daughter. The Gentiles were to remain outside the context of the teachings of Jesus; for them were left only the crumbs ($\tau\grave{a}$ $\psi\iota\chi\acute{\iota}a$). But for these very Jewish disciples the stumbling block came when they had to view their Master crucified as a common criminal; this was more than they could bear. Even if they were able to see through all this, how would they testify, or for that matter even face their critics? Their embarrassment continued and the evidence of this remains in the Scriptures.

The church had to face up to the day when there was no longer any living apostle who had known Jesus. The message was still that Jesus' return was imminent. But as time passed, the early Christians became less and less certain that his return was imminent. Now all accounts of Jesus came second- and third-hand, and the people were left puzzled and dejected. The promise was still that he would return, but the most important question was: "How long?" They looked intently for symbols and signs, which they did not receive. This certainly did not stop the onslaught of criticism and scorn. They turned to the Old Testament and to all manner of other sources, vainly seeking their answers. Finally the Apostle John died, cutting them off from the earliest traditions and leaving them simply embarrassed to face tomorrow. The only solution was to reexamine completely their whole theology; since they were unable to do this by themselves, Paul provided the working solution.

Paul started with the most offensive part, namely, the crucifixion, and made it the very center of his gospel. And as he preached Christ and Christ crucified, the most repulsive account in the whole of Judaism, he found at the same time that it was also the most magnetic teaching he had yet encountered. It would appear that the message of the Jerusalem church was doomed to failure; if it had succeeded, it would have come over under the wings of Judaism and perhaps would have lacked both the challenge and the power to establish itself firmly and permanently. Paul's words appealed neither to the Jew nor to the Greek in form, but the inscrutable mystery behind the crucifixion kindled it afresh again and again to all mankind.

Whatever their personal objections to the crucifixion, these early Christians somehow came to stand on the firm conviction that their Master had survived, and in some way they began to see a light through the fog of mystery and the darkness of doubt. Perhaps, too, they looked to the letters of Paul for a theology to lift them to the beyond. The account of the Ethiopian eunuch raised the problem that the crucifixion was indeed a tragic misfortune due merely to the sheer ignorance of their own Jewish leaders; they had hoped that it was Jesus who would redeem Israel. However, Jesus' followers took comfort and refuge in the fact that these events had been foretold and it was only by these means that Jesus was able to attain true messiahship. Was it by accident or by design that the eunuch happened to pick up the messianic portrait of the Suffering Servant of Yahweh? This is the first direct instance of the identification of Jesus with the Suffering Servant.

Closer scrutiny will certainly indicate that this passage was hand-tailored to avoid the connections with the sins of others in regard to the death of the victim. This conveniently took the problem out of the hands of the Jerusalem Jews and safely vested it in the Old Testament tradition, which was beyond contradiction. Since the fate of Jesus was now placed on the level of preexistence, it also would remove any of the residual guilt that the Jerusalem Jews might have felt, and therefore this theme took the foremost position in the apologetic of the Jerusalem Christians. This having been solved, it became a dead issue and they immediately turned their complete attention to the second coming of Christ. Thus, at an early stage their thought moved from the crucifixion to Jesus' second coming since this seemed the only way out of a tremendous problem.

The general attitude toward personal soteriology in the time of Paul was like the Old Jewish concept in which the Jew stood morally responsible to God and eventually would have to reveal a strict account to either God or the Messiah for all his actions. There was to be a resurrection of the soul and body restoring man to his complete nature, excluding physical deformities where needed. The thinking-out of the position of the Gentiles is not altogether clear; however, one can safely conclude that the scheme was basically for the Jews—the Gentiles were left out.

Paul's epistles were written to express his theology on certain prescribed issues that troubled the early church, and any insights one might glean concerning his anthropology come only by way of inference. Consequently, Paul's letters do not contain any systematic approach to man and his potential, his physical or spiritual abilities, or any insight into his personality. There is no defined, clear-cut doctrine with regard to the relationship of body and soul. His theme is simply one of God's salvation brought through the work and life of Christ. And since this is the background of all his thoughts, even insofar as they relate to contemporary difficulties among the existing churches, the concepts of man are merely tangent to his theme. Paul is inconsistent in even the little view of man in which he sees him as being both dichotomous and trichotomous (1 Thess. 5:23). Man's nature in this incident happens to be merely a sideline to the theology that Paul had in mind. Therefore, he was not concerned because he did express this rift—both views were contained in contemporary Hebrew thought.

The following statements can be made in regard to Paul's concept of man:

1. Resurrection had meaning for Paul only within the context of a body. However, he never meant to infer that it would be merely a continuation of this bodily existence. His concept was one of continuity rather than continuation; he spoke of a "spiritual body" (1 Cor. 15:44) or a "glorious body" (Phil. 3:21). This was never to be confused with the immortality of the soul, which took on no bodily existence. The body was always viewed as part of man's creaturehood. Without it he could not exist as a being, albeit it would have to meet the specifications of its new existence.

2. Paul would never have attacked fornication as related in 1 Corinthians 6:12-20 if he could have conceived of body and soul as being two distinct entities. The Greeks did have a dual morality system because they believed that sexual promiscuity did in no case affect their spiritual side. As long as the two elements could be completely divorced from each other, they could exist in complete moral schizophrenia. But Paul saw that body and soul were completely integrated internally as well as externally; the actions of one had severe and continued influence on the other. The difficulty at Corinth arose out of the failure to understand or appreciate the difference between the Hebrew concept of personality and the Platonic dualism. Man's concept of himself as a being ultimately raises various aspects of his nature and destiny.

With this radical difference in the background, the confusion that followed could not be avoided. The Greek view was obviously used to rationalize sexual libertinism,

as was done later in certain Gnostic circles: fornication can be considered as an adiaphoron which does not essentially threaten the purity of the divine soul. In contrast with this Paul emphasizes the fact that what a human being does with his body does not only affect the physical side of life but his whole being. Hence Paul exhorts the members of the Church to remember that: "your body is a temple of the Holy Spirit within you, which you have from God. You are not your own; you were bought with a price. So glorify God in your body."[2]

Paul never attempted to praise or glorify the body at the expense of the soul, or vice versa. Therefore, they are indispensable to each other and in fact indistinguishable. Paul never used the word *psyche* in those passages dealing with his beliefs on the future life. One might counter that, though it is not mentioned, it is certainly inferred. However, the fact remains that Paul nowhere mentioned *psyche* in this context (2 Cor. 5:1-10; Phil. 1:23). Then death is not viewed as the long-expected liberator but rather as the ultimate in evil which reigns over both body and soul.

Paul's difficulties with the early church can be seen most clearly in the letter to the Galatians. He felt impelled to speak of these differences between himself and the Jerusalem church with regard to the nature and the mission of Jesus. He at first felt called upon to defend his own position as one, in this instance, correcting the church. His revelation came not after man or even from man but rather through the revelation of Jesus Christ (Gal. 1:11-12). There is no human element in this; consequently, there is no opportunity for human error. On the one hand, Paul claimed to be an apostle having full and equal status with all others; yet on the other hand, he claimed that he spoke quite independently from all others by the nature of his special revelation (Gal. 1:15-17). He maintained that God had called him for the special and specific purpose of bringing in Gentiles so that they might understand and believe. His theology must have been different from that of those who were presenting Christ to the Jews, or else there would have been no need for his calling.

Yet, Paul did not see this as a violation of principles because he had been ordained to do this. Could his mind rest knowing that what he was doing was different from what perhaps anyone else was doing? And as he asked later: "Are there two gospels?" Paul did not feel under a heavy sense of obligation to the church of Jerusalem since it was not responsible for his conversion. In fact, it may have in truth detracted him from Christianity. His reaction to the early church was one of utter violence and he sought to do away with it entirely. The answer may be found in the First Letter of Paul to the Corinthians (22-23): "For Jews demand signs . . . but we preach Christ crucified, a stumbling block (σκάνδαλον) to Jews. . . ." "The *skandalon* here resides in the expression Χριστὸν ἐσταυρωμένον— 'a crucified Messiah'. As we have seen, the Crucifixion had been a *skandalon* to the original disciples, who had only surmounted it by the force of their own spiritual experience and explained it by their invocation of the prophecy concerning the Suffering Servant in *Isaiah*."[3] This, however, did not answer the problem for Paul. He saw it as an easy solution to a far more complex problem. Standing in the tradition of the Hebrew fathers, Paul still saw the crucifixion as a *skandalon,* "when in the Galatian Epistle he specially sets forth his exegesis of the *Torah* injunction: 'Cursed is every one that hangeth on a tree.' "[4]

Though one shall never know the form or the content of Paul's conversion, one may have to conclude that to Paul it meant that Jesus did survive death and thus functioned in his own life. But this was no easy matter since he had to reexamine all his thinking in terms of this one profound experience. He now found himself in the embarrassing position of being cast in the lot of the disciples, certain that he was an outsider in both thought and deed. This must have been a most traumatic experience for Paul, and one that raised many perplexing problems for the church. God, as it were, delivered a most offensive prodigal son at its very doorstep. If this was not enough, Paul maintained that he was independent of its authority and challenged the church's traditions. It must have appeared to him that he was an apostle to the Gentiles more out of expediency than divine necessity.

"How then did he surmount the *skandalon* of the Crucifixion? Not by explaining it away, as did the original disciples, but by perceiving therein a divine mystery, the logic of which revolutionised the original form of Christianity by transforming it into a soteriological faith of universal relevance. Accordingly, the Crucifixion was put in the forefront of Paul's gospel."[5] The disciples took the crucifixion and hid it and belittled it. But not Paul, for he proceeded to lift it out of the specific historical context and then reintroduce it in his own esoteric concepts.

Howbeit we speak wisdom among the perfect [the Greek word τέλειος in this context surely has a mystery-religion connotation]: yet a wisdom not of this *aiōn*, nor of the rulers of this *aiōn* (οὐδὲ τῶν ἀρχόντων τοῦ αἰῶνος τούτου), who are becoming nonentities: but we speak God's wisdom in a mystery (ἐν μυστηρίῳ), the hidden wisdom, which God foreordained before the *aiōnes* unto our glory, which none of the rulers of this *aiōn* knoweth: for had they known it, they would not have crucified the Lord of glory (I Cor. 2:6-8).[6]

By this means of transplantation, the crucifixion became a part of God's preexisting plan. It was known to God before the beginning of creation and hence became a part of his plan of creation. There is contained within this the concept of the universe, a being in constant struggle with the forces of the demonic, who is attempting to thwart God's plan and purpose.

Again we see in the Letter of Paul to the Colossians (1:13-19) that Paul designates the Son, who for him was Christ, as veritable *deuteros theos*. Christ has won out in victory over the ordinances that were against us and defeated the principalities and powers (Col. 2:14-15). Although there can be no final exegesis of these passages, again it must be seen that there is the struggle with the demonic forces which were answered in the crucifixion. This power stemming from the universe is seen in Paul's writings (Col. 2:8, 20), in which he infers that the "elemental spirits," meaning the planets and the stars, give rise to understanding only the popular religious and philosophical ideals of their day. "Accordingly, we see Paul regarding the

Christian disciple's mystical identification with Christ in his death as effecting some kind of delivery or emancipation from the celestial bodies of the universe."[7]

Further confirmation of this view is seen in the Letter of Paul to the Galatians, in another context. He maintains that they are under bondage to the rudiments of the world, having been released only in the fullness of time through God's Son (Gal. 4:3-4). He asks how, after one comes to the knowledge of God, he can then turn back to the weak and beggarly rudiments (Gal. 4:8-11). This astral element lifted the conflict of powers from the plains of daily existence and placed it securely in the celestial realms. This then constituted the background of Paul's working reference for the *mythos* of salvation. Man had existed under the powers of the demonic, which were of cosmic dimension, and was in bondage to them. But from the very beginning God planned to release him by his power in sending his Son to become incarnate and then crucified in order to deceive and defeat the evil forces.

From this one can discern that the whole of history is working toward God's salvation, which has already been revealed in Christ. Hence, the name "salvation history" is applied to Paul's concept. Though the process was preexistent in God's mind, and though it was begun and indeed became visible in Christ's life, its true fruition must wait upon the world to come. By means of tieing past, present, and future together Paul effectively bound Jewish, Jerusalem Christian, and his own thoughts together, crystallizing and strengthening them for a much wider worldly appeal. Since these divine events had already begun in the life, death, and resurrection of Jesus Christ, they were represented in the whole "past" of history. And since the future was filled with earnest and eager expectation of the completion of history, Paul believed that the "here and now" of earthly existence became by far the most important aspect for all mankind.

Life, then, is viewed as being transitory, lasting for only the interim period which passes before we know it. The imminence of the end is a binding force in our lives and in the entire community of the church. Life too is bathed in "salvation history," which has begun and continues to move rapidly to its fulfillment. This was a part of Paul's faith which he saw "in a mirror dimly." And since his concept of "salvation history" was so essential to his thought and his whole theme was centered and worked about it, all that he was to say of life, death, or the future was an intricate part of this. One's death and destiny are linked because of his beliefs. Thus, when some of the members of the church in Corinth rejected the teaching of the resurrection, Paul fired back at them in chapter 15 of First Corinthians.

An entirely new situation came out of the resurrection of Christ. By his death he rang in a new age. Just as all the descendants of Adam shared in the certain death of inheritance, so through Christ all shall be made alive. The resurrection of Christ ushered in a new age of a new world (1 Cor. 15:20-22). As one being first born from the dead, he gave rise to a new expectation and an intensely deepened relationship with the Father. All of this was new because it was centered on the resurrection of Christ as the final guarantor.

It is easily seen how dominant and indeed domineering the creed of the resurrection became for Paul by sheer weight, if one only examines a short précis of his theology. It is apparent that Paul was never far from the resurrection in his writings or his preaching.

He addresses himself to the unfaithful Galatians as "Paul an apostle—not from men nor through man, but through Jesus Christ and God the Father, who raised him from the dead" (Gal. 1:1 [an attribute of God no less!]). When informing the Romans of the tenor of his preachings, he refers to these at the beginning of his letter as "the gospel concerning his Son, who was descended from David according to the flesh and designated son of God in power according to the Spirit of holiness by his resurrection from the dead, Jesus Christ our Lord" (Rom. 1:3, 4). Further on in the same epistle he is able to define himself and the Church of Christ thus: "us [we] who believe in him that raised from the dead Jesus our Lord, who was put to death for our trespasses and raised for our justification" (Rom. 4:24, 25). This belief in the resurrection is no mere lip service, it springs from the heart (Rom. 10:9) as is witnessed by the Apostle's own life.

If Christ had not been raised, then there would be no resurrection of the dead either, and all Paul's struggles with the threat of death before him would have been in vain (I Cor. 15:32). After having been in such great peril in Asia that he despaired of his life and felt as if he had already received his death sentence, he realizes that all this was "to make us rely not on ourselves but on God who raises the dead" (2 Cor. 1:9).[8]

The present for Paul was to be accepted in faith as being only a portion of salvation, looking continually to the fulfillment of salvation which would come at the end of things. While there is the assurance in Paul's writings that Christ has ultimately defeated evil and death on the cross and through the resurrection, nevertheless the demonic still has a tenacious and lasting grip on the world of men. There will continually be this cosmic struggle, but Christians can proceed with the assurance that they are joining forces with the winning side because of what Christ did through the resurrection. Still, the whole of creation continues to groan and travail until God has completed his waiting and then reveals the true Son of God. While liberty in this world is only partial, those who have begun to taste freedom long and cry out for its completion. It is only when Christ comes again in power that all dominion will be given over completely to God (1 Cor. 15:24-28).

Salvation has entered into the world and is working toward the end that Christ will come again. There will be the resurrection of the dead, followed by the last judgment, and concluded when God becomes all in all. This is the constant vision that Paul found behind his whole concept of life and what he believed would happen after death. From these basic concepts Paul did not change one iota. While he continued to mature in faith and insight, the very core of his kerygma continued as a constant.

Professor J. N. Sevenster believes that the history of salvation in regard to the fulfillment in the second coming, the resurrection of the dead, and the last judgment, was and always remained the very core of Paul's eschatological expectation. Sevenster further maintains that Hellenistic ideas never swayed or colored Paul's views concerning the doctrines of the last things. Even in those letters which come closest to Hellenistic thought, Paul did not waver from his original thoughts concerning the resurrection and the last judgment.

He himself declares that his experiences, whereby he has been closely confronted with the possibility of dying, have obliged him to "rely not on [himself] but on God who raises the dead" (2 Cor. 1:9). Accordingly there is nothing to prove that the threat of death has brought about any alteration in his expectations. In this letter, too, as in all his letters, he refers to the coming day of the Lord (2 Cor. 1:14). Even in the pericope in which Hellenistic notions have often been claimed to be present, he writes in complete agreement with what has always formed the centre of his expectations: "We must all appear before the judgment seat of Christ, so that each one may receive good or evil, according to what he has done in the body" (2 Cor. 5:10). In the same letter he affirms: "he who raised the Lord Jesus will raise us also with Jesus and bring us with you into his presence" (2 Cor. 4:14). All four chapters of his letter to the Philippians also contain clear references to his expectation that God "will bring to completion at the day of Jesus Christ" the good work that He has begun (Phil. 1:6; cf. 1:10; 2:16), that there will be a resurrection of the dead (3:11), that Jesus "who will change our lowly body to be like his glorious body" will return from heaven.[9]

This empirical faith is what Paul believed to be the entirely new element in the lives of the Gentile converts to Christ. Without the knowledge of God's revelation through Christ, they were like ones "having no hope and without God in the world" (Eph. 2:12). After having been transformed, they could face life knowing that the problem of death was no longer the same as for those who "have no hope" (1 Thess. 4:13).

It is only in and through this same hope that Paul dared to venture forth into the world proclaiming the message of Christ and Christ crucified. Paul did not for a moment assert that he held all the answers, for he tells us that he was cast down and perplexed on every side. Yet, he did have the working solution to death, and he did not need to face this tremendous problem alone or in desperation. There were never any kind words for death on Paul's lips because it stood diametrically opposed to God and his plans. Death was the ultimate in evil, yet before the power of God even death had to quiver.

For Paul death is not the moment when the spirit is released from the fetters of the body; it is not the natural transition to another state, which takes place so spontaneously and gradually that it should arouse no fear whatsoever; it is not the natural consequence of a law of nature. Paul would not contemplate saying that death has nothing terrifying in itself, or that life is made dear to us by the boon and mercy of death, that death might be called "the most precious discovery of Nature", *optimum inventum naturae.* On the contrary, for him death without Christ, "the hope of glory" (Col. 1:27), is an enemy which has been able to force its way into God's universe. . . . Death is not natural, but unnatural in God's universe. It really has no place therein. Hence it can never become a kind and merciful friend; it would always have remained a feared enemy if Jesus Christ had not risen, if this had not deprived death of all hope of an ultimate victory, and removed death's sting, if Christ had not dethroned the last enemy, death, once and for all (I Cor. 15:55, 26).[10]

However, it was only with these beliefs firmly rooted that Paul was bold to say that for him dying could be gain (Phil. 1:21).

The word Paul uses here for "gain" *(kerdos),* is used twice by Socrates in the *Apology,* in the belief that he can deprive death of its fearfulness by representing it as a probably dreamless sleep *(Apol.* 40, d, e). Paul knows of no other reason for calling death a gain than the fact of the victory over death which has already taken place, and which will in time lead to a complete conquest. Without this victory death would not be a good, an adiaphoron: it would be impossible to imagine a worse evil than death. That Paul now and then expresses the desire to depart this world arises from his knowledge that he would then be with Christ, which is preferable by far (Phil. 1:23). Death is dominated by the idea of "being with the Lord": "So we are always of good courage; we know that while we are at home in the body we are away from the Lord, for we walk by faith, not by sight. We are of good courage, and we would rather be away from the body and at home with the Lord (2 Cor. 5:6-8)."[11]

It would be hard to assume from this that Paul could look directly upon death as being a gain; it is better to assume that he was looking past the intervention of death to the glory beyond. Death for Jesus or even for himself was neither attractive nor necessarily a positive gain. The early church bore witness to this and he would also. But beyond the experience of death he would be at one "with Christ" in a newer, deeper, more intimate way than he ever knew possible, which certainly held more for him than any aspect of this life. And so in order to be "with the Lord" Paul could look past this life to the life to come in power and in fullness when he would never be separated from the Lord.

There is here no sense of escapism or liberation because in a real sense he had "died" in his conversion. He had become a "new man" and already had given himself over to death. Thus, he could look forward to the day when he would come into his full reality and put away all the consequential limits that this creation imposed on both his body and soul. A case cannot be made from his writings that he could ever envisage death as a separation of body and soul. In fact, the word *soul* was never used when Paul spoke in terms of expectation. He may have believed that in the interim period between death and the final resurrection the soul might exist empty of form.

As Paul grew older it appears that he saw a rather long period existing between death and the resurrection (1 Thess. 4:15-18). Man thus stands in apparent nakedness (2 Cor. 5:3), meaning, to Paul, individuals without bodies. This would not be in any sense the full complement of man and left much to be desired. Paul's thought here is in tune with the whole of the primitive church, which believed that in this interim period the individual would be subjected to sleep. "The idea of a temporary state of waiting is all the more repugnant to those who would like fuller information about this 'sleep' of the dead who, though stripped of their fleshly bodies, are still deprived of their resurrection bodies although in possession of the Holy Spirit. They are not able to observe the discretion of the New Testament authors, including St Paul, in this matter; or to be satisfied with the joyful assurance of the Apostle when he says that henceforth death can no longer separate from Christ him who has the Holy Spirit. 'Whether we live or die, we belong to Christ.' "[12]

The basic difficulty comes when we fail to realize that this is an analogy, and as such must fail as an analogy. Certainly Paul did not know exactly how one would come through the experience, and no matter how clairvoyant he may have been, he could never relate the sensations as such. The difficulty comes not because we sleep, but rather because we really might not sleep. But whether one would be with Christ immediately or only after a long time was not really a valid question in Paul's sight. He knew that ultimately he would be with Christ. Whether he would be transformed in a moment or at the end of time, to Paul it was all the same. Yet, however he may have rationalized the time sequence, there is absolutely no doubt that he hoped that it would be soon. He looked forward to the time when his body would be transformed and then he would be made whole (2 Cor. 5:2-4).

This represents a radical and basic contrast with the beliefs of the Greek philosophers. They and Paul were looking for two different things. The Greeks looked for separation as the ultimate goal, whereas Paul looked to complete integration as being the only true freedom.

What Seneca finds so desirable in death, is for Paul the temporary state of "nakedness", which he wishes to be as brief as possible and from which he apparently recoils. While what Paul longs for with all the ardour of his faith, the resurrection of the dead in a new spiritual, transfigured body, would strike Seneca as a relapse into a state which death had finally superseded. Here too it is clear that "der Eschatologe muss fast alle seine theologischen Geheimnisse verraten." In expressing their views on the after-life, both Paul and Seneca disclose the mysteries of their doctrine concerning God and man, and in so doing also reveal their soteriology.[13]

Wherever one begins with Paul's doctrine of the death of Christ, he must realize that this was not merely his theology—it was his gospel. "It is not possible to argue that the death of Christ has less than a central, if not the central and fundamental place, in the apostle's gospel."[14] It was continually present and foremost in all his actions, meditations, and deeds. Paul wrote in his letter to the Galatians: "Even if we, or an angel from heaven, should preach to you a gospel contrary to that which we preached to you, let him be accursed. As we have said before, so now I say again, If any one is preaching to you a gospel contrary to that which you received, let him be accursed" (Gal. 1:8-9). Professor Denney assumes that Paul was arguing a case for religious intolerance in this passage.

The point at issue between the apostle and his Jewish Christian adversaries was not whether Christ had died for sins; every Christian believed that. It was rather how far this death of Christ reached in the way of producing or explaining the Christian life. To Paul it reached the whole way. It explained everything; it supplanted everything he could call a righteousness of his own; it inspired everything he could call righteousness at all. To his opponents, it did not so much supplant as supplement. . . . It is not necessary to enter into this controversy here . . . underneath the controversy Paul and his opponents agreed in the common Christian interpretation of Christ's death as a death in which sin had been so dealt with that it no longer barred fellowship between God and those who believed in Jesus.[15]

We must be continually aware that the epistles were written over a period of some fifteen years. We cannot assume that after the experience on the Damascus Road there was a Pauline theology any more than we can assume that there was a New Testament theology in New Testament times. Paul did not come upon his theology in full bloom; it had to be nourished, cultured, and occasionally pruned. Therefore, one cannot assume that the theology of his first letters is necessarily consistent with the theology in his latter manuscripts. Yet, he remains so consistent with the nature and the meaning of Christ's death that, systematically, one cannot discern one letter from another. "The apostle had one message on Christ's death from first to last of his Christian career. His gospel, and it was the only gospel he knew, was always 'the word of the cross' (1 Cor. 1:18), or 'the word of reconciliation' (2 Cor. 5:19). The applications might be infinitely varied, for, as has been already pointed out, everything was involved in it, and the whole of Christianity was deduced from it; but this is not to say that it was in process of evolution itself."[16] While certainly the facts and the nature of the death of Christ were constant and unchanging, there is no reason to assume that Paul's own personal attitudes could not evolve. In fact they did, and this does not detract one iota from the nature of Christianity.

Paul's view of death and eschatology was much different from the view of those who stand in the mainstream of Protestant theology. "The tradition of Protestant theology undoubtedly tends to isolate the death, and to think of it as a thing by itself, apart from the resurrection; sometimes, one is tempted to say, apart even from any distinct conception of Him who died."[17] Paul always saw that there was an indestructible bond between Christ's death and his resurrection. Few people have ever attempted to raise the resurrection to the heights of theology as Paul did. At times he related it exactly: "we believe that Jesus died and rose again" (1 Thess. 4:14), on which hinges the whole Christian faith. In Romans the resurrection and the death are combined equally. Jesus "was put to death for our trespasses and raised for our justification" (Rom. 4:25). This distillation of truths appears again in the First Letter of Paul to the Corinthians: ". . . of first importance [is] that Christ died for our sins in accordance with the scriptures, that he was buried, that he was raised on the third day in accordance with the scriptures" (1 Cor. 15:3-4). But there are other places in which the emphasis falls completely on the resurrection. Paul writes, ". . . if you confess with your lips that Jesus is Lord and believe in your heart that God raised him from the dead, you will be saved" (Rom. 10:9). The same standard returns in, "If Christ has not been raised, your faith is futile and you are still in your sins" (1 Cor. 15:17).

Then why did Paul have such an ungainly view of the resurrection? This, of course, can be seen only in the historical context of the individual himself.

It was the appearance of the risen One to Paul which made him a Christian. What was revealed to him on the way to Damascus was that the crucified One was the Son of God, and the gospel that He preached afterwards was that of the Son of God crucified. There can be no salvation from sin unless there is a living Saviour: this explains the emphasis laid by the apostle on the resurrection. But the living One can be a Saviour only because He has died: this explains the emphasis laid on the cross. The Christian believes in a living Lord, or he could not believe at all; but he believes in a living Lord who died an atoning death, for no other can hold the faith of a soul under the doom of sin.[18]

It is from this sustained dynamic relationship with the Christ who returned from the dead that Paul received his drive and power.

How, then, did Paul proceed to define his gospel? How did he work it out in the known context of the existing forms of the church and established religion? He first began in the context of God's nature. "Ever since the creation of the world his invisible nature, namely, his eternal power and deity, has been clearly perceived in the things that have been made" (Rom. 1:20). But this was not enough. It certainly makes known to all men everywhere God's existence, and something of his divine power, glory, and faithfulness, but if man is to come to know God personally, as Paul did, to have his sins forgiven and to enter into relationship with God, he needs a more intimate and practical revelation. It is only through the divine personal encounter with the living Christ that the believer can really come to understand his holiness, his power to release men from their sins, and especially his love.

This is basically where Paul would separate the Old Testament from the New Testament, because of this fuller knowledge of God's love. Though God spoke of his love through the prophets and the psalmist, men could begin to comprehend his love only through the most vivid demonstration of it—a demonstration that would be etched on their minds and hearts so that it could never be forgotten, something never to be excelled, nothing short of *a unique act*. Every man is occasionally touched by the good act or word of another, but God's act must completely transcend and surpass all such human actions. "One will hardly die for a righteous man—though perhaps for a good man one will dare even to die. But God shows his love for us in that while we were yet sinners Christ died for us" (Rom. 5:7-8). Here then is Paul's basic theme: the only true interpretation one can have of Christ's death is through God's love. And however Paul may approach the death of Christ, he is always consistent with the expression of God's love through Christ's death. For Paul it is then the love of God with which all other theological convictions must be reconciled.

The other aspect of the death of Christ is the love of Christ himself. Paul makes numerous references to this, among which are: ". . . I live by faith in the Son of God, who loved me and gave himself for me" (Gal. 2:20). "The love of Christ controls us, because we are convinced that one has died for all" (2 Cor. 5:14). ". . . Christ loved the church and gave himself up for her" (Eph. 5:25). Christ here is not some cold, mechanical entity but rather an individual who opens himself as a vehicle for God's will.

The motive in which God acts is the motive in which He (Christ) acts: the Father and the Son are at one in the work of man's salvation. It is this which is expressed when the work of Christ is described, as it is in Phil. 2:8 and Rom. 5:19, as obedience—obedience unto death, and that the death of the cross. The obedience is conceived as obedience to the loving will of the Father to save men—that is, it is obedience in the vocation of Redeemer, which involves death for sin. It is not obedience merely in the sense of doing the will of God as other men are called to do it, the everyday keeping of God's commandments; it is obedience in this unique and incommunicable, yet moral, calling to be at the cost of life the Saviour of the world from sin. Hence it is in the obedience of Christ to the Father that the great demonstration of *His* love to men is given; "He loved me," the apostle says, "and gave Himself for me."[19]

It is in this manner that Christ could move forward to the cross as the means of fullest obedience measured out in depth only by his own death.

But what then is Christ's death in relation to sin? First and foremost Paul saw Christ's death as a death for sin. It was sin that caused God to enter this world in the person of Christ, and it was sin that made Christ's death a necessity in order to reveal God's love as well as Christ's. It was only by sin that death held any power over us and it was only by wrestling with evil that Jesus could effectually accept our responsibility—and die for us.

It is easy to look upon death as being something quite natural, because all living things do in fact die. Yet, on the other hand, there is still much about death that is offensive and unnatural. It is the unnatural aspect with which the Christian faith deals. Although death can be explained by all manner of natural phenomena, it still does not "touch the profounder truth with which Paul is dealing, that death comes from God, and that it comes in man to a being who is under law to Him. Man is not like a plant or an animal, nor is death to him what it is at the lower levels of life. Man has a moral nature in which there is a reflection of the holy law of God, and everything that befalls him, including death itself, must be interpreted in relation to that nature."[20]

However, according to the apostle, God's view is that death is the wages of sin. "The connection between sin and death is real, though it is not physical; and because it is what it is, because death by God's ordinance has in the conscience of sinful men the tremendous significance which it does have, because it is a power by which they are all their lifetime held in bondage, because it is the expression of God's implacable and final opposition to evil, He who came to bear our sin must also die our death. Death is the word which sums up the whole liability of man in relation to sin, and therefore, when Christ came to give Himself for our sins, He did it by dying."[21]

It was the divine encounter with Christ which left Paul no choice but to reconsider the Jesus of history. He stood at the end of Christ's life and had to reshape Christ's entire life from entirely new criteria, all of which became transformed and developed into depth of spirit and thought for Paul. It was not so much the crucifixion that offended him as it was the curse of the Torah which proclaimed that one hung on a tree defiled the land henceforth. Paul could not conceive of Jesus as a means of defilement. But through the Spirit the cross was transformed " 'from the wooden instrument of a dreamer's death to the supreme altar of the Christian Faith'."[22]

The Acts of the Apostles maintain that it was the fulfillment of God's purposes through scripture. However, William Manson is right when he says, " 'for the evidence of a more inward appreciation of the meaning of the Messiah's death we have . . . to look away from Acts to St. Paul'."[23] One cannot make the erroneous assumption that Paul was the only Christian thinker wrestling with the truths of Christ's life.

On the contrary Paul himself has specially asserted that he owed to the Church a particular interpretation of the Death of Jesus [1 Corinthians 15:3]. . . . Paul shared in what might be called a treasury of thought on the Death of Jesus which was common in varying degrees to all Christians, and that he applied to that event certain interpretations that were current coin, as it were, in the primitive Church. To judge from the wealth of material presented to us on this subject by the various Epistles of the New Testament the Church must have become increasingly Cross-conscious . . . and markedly individual as is much of Paul's thought on the Death of Jesus, it developed against the background of a Church that was wrestling with the same problem.[24]

Paul so took this rich inheritance and molded it to his own concepts that he in fact did become an innovator.

The death of Jesus for the Jew must always be seen against a background of sacrifice. Our culture has moved so far from this tradition that it is not only incomprehensible but deeply offensive. However, for the Jew it was the necessary and proper approach to God. The death of Christ and the new life were like two focuses of an ellipse being held together by the concept of "blood" which had been sacrificed. To the Hebrew mind there could never be atonement without sacrifice—sacrifice involving the shedding of blood.

W. D. Davies, following C. H. Dodd, maintains that *ilasterion* means "expiation" not "propitiation," resulting in the Christian counterpart of the Jewish *kapporeth*. Further, Davies maintains that since First Corinthians was written before the Passover season, the terms and thoughts of its ritual were definitely on Paul's mind.[25] For example, in 1 Corinthians 15:23 and 5:7 references are made to first fruits and elements of ritual. While these need not be correlated exactly to the Christian faith, it has been the task of Christian apologists to transform older symbols and rituals into newer and more appropriate meanings.

Paul then viewed the Last Supper as the covenant relationship sealed by the blood of Christ and set this forth as being central to his message. He gathered up the traditions about the early church and made them definite and complete. Jesus, standing in the Jewish tradition, must also have seen the Last Supper as a means of instituting a covenant relationship. And while Paul gathered these elements from the church, they were viewed through traditional rabbinic eyes.

We cannot discuss here the significance of the covenant and its ramifications, but it is important that the nature of obedience be examined. Through a covenant an individual found himself in a special relationship to God, and he could continue this relationship only by his response of obedience.

In Paul's opinion, supreme obedience could best be shown through martyrdom. Perhaps this shows a high regard for the Hasidim, who placed the highest value on obedience even to death. To Paul the death of Jesus meant an act of obedience to the complete will of God. Whereas in all Old Testament sacrifice the umblemished lamb was led to the slaughter, the compelling thing about Jesus was his personal choice. It came as the highest form of sacrifice because the participant had freedom of choice. Paul raised these factors in 2 Corinthians 10:5, Romans 5:13-18, and Philippians 2:8, which provide the clue that he saw this in terms of rabbinic thought. Here for Paul the concept of obedience is primary. In the Letter to the Hebrews, sacrifice is the primary factor as opposed to Romans (5:17-19).

So the death of Jesus was seen through very rabbinic eyes and rested in the familiar patterns and thoughts of rabbinic Judaism. Paul saw Jesus not only as one who fulfilled his obedience completely (Phil. 2:5-11) but also as the Messiah, the Suffering Servant of Deutero-Isaiah.

If our thesis be correct, the suffering of Jesus as Messiah would not in itself be an insuperable difficulty for a Rabbi such as Paul, at least it would probably have been less difficult for him than for simpler folk who had perhaps less refined conceptions of the Messianic Kingdom than the Rabbis. Nevertheless, we do know that there was a *skandalon* for Paul in the Death of Jesus and we now suggest that even if Judaism did not expect a Suffering Messiah at all, the chief cause of the element of *skandalon* in the Death of Jesus for Paul was not the Death in itself but the form which it took; it was the death on the Cross that constituted the *skandalon*.[26]

Suffering and death were quite within the realm of possibility, but Paul was too refined and too serious a respecter of the Torah not to be upset by the difficulties of the cross. This was almost more than the rabbis could either accept or comprehend. Time has so removed us from their minds and traditions that we shall never measure the depth with which this *skandalon* resounded.

Paul's eschatology is ever so much more difficult to study when it is dissected at the end as if it were some vestigial organ. As long as there continues to be the strong and serious rift in theology and eschatology in the thought of Paul, one will never come to grips with his real meaning and importance. Paul could see meaning in the life of Jesus only when he concluded that here was truly the Messiah of old. And as has been previously mentioned, his difficulty did not arise so much from Jesus' failure to fulfill the contemporary expectations as it did from his dying an accursed death. It was only through the refinement of eschatology and application of these criteria to Jesus' teaching and preaching that the pieces began to take their rightful places.

"The encounter with the living Christ, the awareness of living in a new creation, the influx of the Gentiles into the true Israel, the experience of a new moral exodus, the discovery of a New Torah and the advent of the Spirit, all these were for Paul eschatological phenomena."[27] It was indeed Paul's eschatology that permeated all his works and actions, and as such it was always in the foreground of his mind. This then became the norm for the approach to any understanding of Pauline thought.

The early church conceived of its own work as placing

the Jesus of history in the solid context of traditional Jewish thought, but the task was not as simple as that. There were obviously many things that could not be reconciled, and perhaps nothing was more difficult than the changing conception of the kingdom. The earnest Jew still looked forward to this with anxious expectation and continued to live on completely oblivious to the fact that the eternal rule had broken in upon him, for he remained ignorant of it. If Jesus was the Messiah, the end had come in the truest sense of Jewish eschatology; but since it had not come in a majestic, worldly manner, it caught the Jews unaware. To alleviate this general apathy and indifference, it was believed that the Lord Jesus would return soon and at this juncture he would indeed fulfill the grandeur that was his. No doubt there was no one more anxious than Paul to see this come about, for he had visions in his zealous compassion of the complete fulfillment of God's reign. This too was promoted by the people of the early church, who believed in the urgency of the return from their awakening glimpses to their closing prayer of Maranatha (Rev. 22:20).

Paul also took comfort in the early return of Jesus, not only because it was the expectation of the early church but also because it would be the fulfillment of all the Old Testament doctrines and prophecies. The message of the early church caught on and spread with unprecedented speed, allowing Paul in his own time to believe that it had truly gone out into all the world bringing the message to all mankind, beyond his highest hopes and expectations. Also, he came to believe that the forces of evil were building up into a grand *crescendo* for their last assault before utter destruction. All of this reinforced, at least in his own mind, the success of Christianity and the assurance that the return of the Lord would come as quickly and unexpectedly as did Paul's first encounter along that Damascus Road.

However, from his dreams and expectations he was brought back again and again to the daily realities of the Christian churches and their individual problems. Death was taking more than its rightful toll, and individuals who once believed so strongly now had their fears and doubts. Was there no distinction among the dead? Just what relevance did the resurrection have for the individual's death? Try as they might to understand the teaching and preaching of the early evangelists, they remained shaken and anxious. Were they to "sleep" on and miss the Messianic Age, or would they be awakened so that they might share in this also? If you dismiss the resurrection life from the early church, you destroy it, for it must be true that those that came over to Christianity did so because of the consequences and the extension of the resurrection. And when it came to be challenged from within, some no doubt left the community, and the church was confronted with its first and longest crisis, which centered on the meaning of the resurrection for their own lives and deaths.

It is a mistake to believe that Paul's thought tied in exactly to the apocalyptic concepts of his day. "That, in his eschatology, the Apostle drew upon the latter for his terms will be obvious, but the character of that eschatology was determined not by any traditional scheme but by that significance which Paul had been led to give to Jesus. This is merely to affirm that his eschatology was subservient to his faith and not constitutive of it."[28] It was Paul's task to take meaningful and significant current religious terminology and translate it into the forms and the context of Christianity. This is the vehicle of expression for all religious entrepreneurs, that is, to take over the existing forms and give them new functions. It is a change in content without a change in terminology.

Paul conveyed to the Christians at Thessalonica that those who had become one "in Christ" were thus transformed into the resurrection mode, which came upon them without entering into the experience of death. Again in Romans (6:1-14) he maintains that out of the union with Christ, who had brought life to all followers, they had already passed from death to life. It was for these individuals that death now became an impossibility. But it is difficult to believe that Paul is saying that people will not die, for this was precisely the problem that he was facing and it would thus become a matter of arguing in circles. Paul seems to be saying that while the forms of death persist, for those "in Christ" the function is different.

In another passage (1 Cor. 11:27-34) Paul suggests that the death of a Christian was a sign of moral failure.

. . . but in I Thessalonians, writing to a Church that was strangely agitated by this problem, Paul has to reassure his fellow-Christians that at the advent of Christ those Christians who had died would be raised so as to share in the same privileges as those who had survived. There is no need to postulate that Paul here introduces the belief in a twofold resurrection under pressure from the logic of Jewish apocalyptic [thought]. On the contrary, the situation that confronted him at Thessalonica was the natural outcome of his own preaching.[29]

W. D. Davies further illuminates this by quoting Héring: " 'We do not err in affirming that Paul himself at an early period had expressly denied the future resurrection and that the anti-resurrectionists at Thessalonica and Corinth were after all only the representatives of the unchanged Pauline belief. It is no less true that their position was strongly placed in line with the fundamental conceptions of the Apostle—a fact which explains both their influence and the difficulty that Paul had to convince them.' "[30]

Whether or not as individuals we adopt this solution, we are brought to the belief that the entire church, as well as Paul, did change its outlook on the resurrection and also death for the individual. It thus follows that Paul was revamping his ideas during the course of writing his letters. Since he never had the entire corpus before him at one time, there was no opportunity to correct himself except by expressing his new beliefs at a later period. However, as it happened, these newer insights were not always addressed to the community that raised the problem in the first instance. Thus, it is quite feasible that at these Pauline communities various views on the same problem were held at the same time, but all had a common denominator—Pauline theology. This can become most confusing and to a certain extent disillusioning, but in the last analysis the essence of the basic dogmas was not in flux. Paul attempted to bring into sharper focus some of the fuzzier details.

This being the case, Paul's basic theology and eschatology

were much simpler than latter-day scholars would lead us to believe. "It contains no reference to a Messianic Kingdom such as is contemplated in Baruch, 4 Ezra, and Revelation and can be briefly summarized as the early expectation of the Parousia when there would be a final judgement, a general resurrection of the righteous dead (and possibly of all the dead), the transformation of the righteous living and ensuing upon all this the final consummation, the perfected Kingdom of God when God would be all in all."[31]

It cannot be emphasized too strongly that Christianity did not come upon a tabula rasa, as also should be made clear with regard to Judaism. The Jews had been looking forward to the belief of resurrection for a long time, and in fact Jesus found great sympathy among the Pharisees because they accepted his teachings on resurrection. Jesus argued from the point of view of their attitudes toward resurrection and never with regard to his own. He was steeped in this tradition, and with this one point of view he had little difficulty. Yet, the Jews did not have to go out of Jerusalem to find the strong Hellenistic views, for they were right there with them. In fact, it can be said that the Talmud is more a monument to Greek philosophy than it is a contribution to Jewish religion. Perhaps nothing else the Greeks gave to the world had greater influence than their gift of the concept of man.

Thus, it was at this juncture that the battle line had to be drawn and maintained. Paul had to call his Christian followers back to the essential Hebrew anthropology. There is an excellent summary of the Jewish position written by Guignebert: " 'The Jews could only conceive of man in his totality, as the vital union of flesh and soul. Their anthropological dichotomy was not dualistic . . . a truly living being was always an embodied spirit, soul and body having been created by God for a mutual interdependence and being therefore incapable of genuine life apart from one another.' "[32]

Death involved an unnatural separation of the body from the soul. Hence, any conception of afterlife must be the reunion and complete integration of these two forms of life. This difficulty not only was perplexing to the Christians but had made marked inroads on Judaism of the first century. "It is clear that there were those who under the influence of Hellenistic conceptions had either modified or abandoned the doctrine of resurrection in favour of the Hellenistic conception of the immortality of the soul."[33] It is easy to understand how this could come about because the Greeks had a much more likely approach. The doctrine of the body still remained a very difficult proposition. No wonder that the Jews who saw the dissolution of their people found it easier to follow the Greek explanation even though it was less sophisticated. It is with such a problem that Paul was challenged to deal in the Corinthian church.

Individuals who were under the Hellenistic influences had difficulty in seeing anything other than a very spiritualized existence.

Resurrection implied that after death the soul departed to Hades or Sheol, and waited there till the day of judgement when it would be reunited to a body. To the educated Hellenistic world, however, such a view of the destiny of the soul was unacceptable on two grounds. First, as Knox has written: "No intelligent and educated person believed in a subterranean Hades; even the authority of Homer and Plato was unable to save it. . . ." And, secondly, as we saw above, it was escape from the body, not any future reunion with it in resurrection, that seemed desirable to the Hellenistic world owing to its particular anthropology.[34]

With this in mind we do not wonder that the Corinthians were bound for difficulties. There is no doubt also that they, like we, reconciled themselves to a bodiless existence and would have been content to let it be. Paul, however, felt that it so diluted the conception of man that he ventured to take issue with them. There is, however, another side to these difficulties, for Paul here was attacking not only the Hellenistic concept of immortality but its converse. There were also the literal interpreters who accepted the physical restoration of the body. It was between these two camps that Paul had to draw the line as to the true Christian conception, realizing that they both contained some of the truth. "In doing this he was not in any way departing from his pharisaic conceptions, because, as we have seen, there would be many Pharisees prepared to argue, as Paul does, for a transformed resurrection body. Moreover, as we have before asserted, we are not too hastily to assume that when Paul speaks of a 'spiritual' body he means thereby an 'immaterial one': the 'spirit' has a physical nuance for Paul such as it often had for his Rabbinic contemporaries. In any case it should be admitted that the 'newness' of Paul's conception of a spiritual mode of resurrection body must not be over-emphasized. . . .''[35]

To R. H. Charles the concept of the "new body" means "successive expressions of the same personality, though in different spheres," and further, Paul points us to the fact that we should receive a new body at death.[36] W. D. Davies maintains that Charles presses the analogy of the seed too far.[37] The essence of a seed is that it may remain dormant for an indefinite time, and it certainly does not follow that one must receive a body immediately at death or else he would be naked. Davies does not acknowledge that the seed contains all that it needs for its transformation. Though to the eye they may all look similar, each seed is unique and already has the contents that will make profound differences. So, too, in the resurrection there must be continuity or the concept becomes absurd, for unless we maintain our essential selves, a future life has no meaning. This would eventually lead to a theory of transmigration of souls. There must be discontinuity in the resurrection since a "physical" continuation of our present existence would handicap us from a deeper and truer fulfillment of life. Thus, one concludes that there can only be a future life that is both continuous and discontinuous. And the degree of such will not be comprehended by our finiteness.

Dr. Albert Schweitzer maintains in his book *The Mysticism of Paul the Apostle* that from the first to the last letter Paul expected the immediate return of Jesus, of judgment and the messianic glory. Further, he maintains that if Paul underwent any change whatsoever, it was not in his eschatological expectation. It would be more accurate if Dr. Schweitzer held that Paul's eschatological themes were constant but the details in fact did change, which will be discussed later.

There is behind all of Paul's eschatological thought the strong thread of redemption. For Paul sees Jesus calling the world to an end and issuing forth the messianic kingdom. This redemption was not only of this world, for it came from outside and beyond this earthly existence. It was a cosmic process which was not invoked by Jesus but rather only announced by him. It was from these factors that the early church had come to see redemption.

Paul could not be considered a promoter of Pharisaism; however, it was from the Pharisees' theology that he was able to see the connection of the two great themes of the reign of the Messiah and the life hereafter. Paul's subjective confrontation had allied him with the intense and intimate religion of the Pharisees. The depths of their religious quest had touched the common ground in his experience. In regard to the concept of salvation, he could not be farther from the Pharisees.

The Jewish solution assumed no sudden entrance of evil into the world, nor any sudden defeat of its power; no total depravity through the sin of Adam, no deliverance through a special agent conceived as both divine and human. It assumed the influence of God slowly working in all human lives, to bring about in the course of ages the harmony which ought to be, between the Creator and His creatures, the Father and His children. There was no other way, if the fundamental facts were as Pharisees and Rabbis believed them to be. But it was the duty of every true servant of God to work with Him towards that great end, by spreading the knowledge of God, and winning men to His service. The end of that gradual process of salvation was far off, how far was known only to God; but its attainment was as certain as that the power and the love of God were sufficient. It did not depend on some sudden exercise of divine power, in a form and through an agent hitherto unknown. The factors remained the same throughout—God and man; and the immeasurable length of the process was due to the infinite complexity of the human lives involved, age after age. The note of hope has, therefore, always sounded in Rabbinical Judaism, in regard to the future of mankind, an unconquerable optimism based on unshakable trust in the goodness and righteousness of God.[38]

In his thought and teachings Jesus could not separate redemption from the cosmic struggle with the demonic. This demonic power is on the increase but will ultimately be defeated. It is as if a strong man has been overcome and bound by yet another, who is even stronger. The first can do nothing as the second lays aside all his works (Matt. 12:22-29). Jesus believed his own death was a means of defeating the "evil one," for this was his role of messiahship. Thus, when Jesus came to his rightful power, he would proceed to cast out all that was alien to God and his purposes for man. Schweitzer feels that it is after the death of John the Baptist that Jesus made his resolution to suffer and die.[39]

Although it is apparent that John's death did recall the seriousness and inevitability of Jesus' own death, it must be assumed that Jesus had set himself to the task earlier, as was discussed in the previous chapter. Even in the Lord's Prayer, we echo this concern of Jesus, that we might be delivered from the "evil one." As Jesus moved closer to death, it became increasingly clear to him that only by his atoning death could the power and the dominion of this "evil one" be broken. Redemption and atonement were intertwined for Jesus; they held a profound and simple meaning for the Jews. Jesus "in His death and resurrection has become the Messiah, will bring in the Kingdom. This explains why the belief of the Early Christians, starting at the death of Jesus, expressed itself in the two parallel assertions that through it He won for Himself exaltation to the Messiahship and also has obtained for His people the forgiveness of their sins. The two apparently disconnected ideas remain, however, in accordance with their origin, attached together by the belief in the nearness of the Kingdom."[40] There is much to be said about the truths that Schweitzer raises here, but one must wonder if his time sequence is proper.

Interestingly enough, it is to Satan that Paul attributes the sufferings of his body. "Because he has been caught up into Heaven and Paradise and has heard things 'which it is not lawful to utter,' he has been delivered up in a special manner to 'the Angel of Satan,' who has authority to buffet him to the end that he may not be exalted overmuch (2 Cor. 12:1-7)."[41]

As Paul envisages the kingdom, he foresees an angelic struggle rather than the peaceful tranquillity which is generally associated with the kingdom. But one by one these apostate forces will come under the sway of Christ and his followers, and at last even death will be robbed of its power (1 Cor. 15:23-28). Death here is considered to be one of the angel powers. This comes from the concept of the Angel of Death in the Apocalypse of Baruch (chap. 21). One cannot discern from this brief source whether the Angel of Death does in fact cause death or if he is merely over those who have died. However, it seems more reasonable that he shares with the demonic and rules from the underworld.

Paul also appears to assume that the Angel of Death not only has power over the dead but also causes death. In I Cor. 15:55 he speaks of the sting of Death. Whether the "Destroyer" to whom, according to I Cor. 10:10, the Israelites who murmured in the wilderness fell a prey is to be identified with the Angel of Death cannot be determined.

The one thing certain is that it is after the overcoming of the Angel of Death that the general Resurrection becomes possible, as is also implied in the Apocalypse of John (Rev. 20:13).[42]

With the defeat of death the curtain is rung down on the messianic kingdom. Paul makes no mention of how long he believes this will last. He expects that Satan will be trodden under foot at the beginning of the messianic kingdom (Rom. 16:20). The reverse is held by John in the Book of Revelation (20:2-3, 7-10), which states that Satan is bound during this messianic period, but he will be released later to rule once more. Then at last, he will be cast into the lake of fire. The whole point of Paul's theme here is that the Messiah has to bow to the authority of the angelic powers. But when he has fought the fight, all will have to render to him his due authority. This must all be done so that at the end, God will prevail and be "all in all." Thus, all of creation will reach its full and complete consummation. Those who have given themselves over to God and have lived by him, are thus united with him with no distinction. Those who have separated themselves from God in this life will be separated from him completely.

Paul conceived of eternal blessedness as more than a spiritual existence and conditioned by the bodily resurrection. The elect have found themselves to be partakers in the messianic kingdom and as such they retain the mode of existence already given in their state of blessedness. "When the condition which, at the Return of Jesus, they receive, either by resurrection or by 'being changed', is spoken of as a condition of incorruption, that means that it is thought of as eternal. What happens is just this, that after a Messianic reign all the dead who at the Judgment are found to be destined to blessedness enter likewise into this condition of imperishable bodily existence."[43]

Into the midst of his conception of blessedness and angelic powers, Paul introduces a new strain which is distinctively his own. This is the conception that the Law was given by angels in order that they might make man subservient to themselves. With the advent of Christ's death their power in and through the Law was broken and as such no longer holds man's allegiance. Therefore, at the beginning of the messianic reign the Law topples from its ancient rule. Yet, in truth Paul sees the Law cancelled by the death of Christ. Paul sees all the miracles and healings that Jesus performed as combating and concluding the evil forces that were opposed to the rule of God.

It is very interesting that Paul must have thought these miracles to be of so little consequence in comparison to the miracle of the resurrection and the ultimate defeat of the demonic that he does not mention them. It is also true that Paul had not seen these events with his own eyes and no doubt did not think it completely right to build his case on them. After all, he started with the very core of Christianity, and if individuals did not accept this, it was unlikely that his case would be any stronger when supported by the miracle stories.

Paul's view on the cancellation of the Law led directly to his tremendous conflict with the early church. The Jews, who were under a heavy sense of obligation to the Law, began to see Jesus as the fulfillment of this Law. On the other hand, there were the Gentiles, who had no concern for and no responsibility to the Law and thus could readily accept Jesus without being bound over to Jewish tradition and Law. The two approaches inevitably led to troubles and discontentment, eventually centered about Paul. The church was fortunate indeed to have a man such as Paul, with his unique background, to calm the raging storms.

Schweitzer believes that the conflict in Pauline eschatology rises out of two converging streams of thought. "It is, in the first place, like the Apocalypses of Baruch and Ezra, a synthesis of the eschatology of the Prophets and of the 'Son-of-Man' eschatology of Daniel; and, in the second place, that it has to reckon with the facts, wholly unforeseen to Jewish eschatology, that the Messiah has already appeared as a man, has died, and is risen again."[44]

Jesus fulfilled the concept of the Son-of-Man eschatology contained in the Books of Daniel and Enoch. He proclaims the coming of the Son of Man; he speaks of himself being surrounded by angels, and sees himself coming in power from the clouds of heaven. His terminology is one of the kingdom of God rather than the messianic kingdom. The thread of Danielic eschatology is picked up and carried out to the fullest expression in Jesus. There was no room within the prophetic eschatology for the conception of martyrdom, and as such it had to give way to the more inclusive and less idealistic Danielic eschatology. The end comes from Daniel and Enoch; "and it is left an open question how far He was directly influenced by these books, and how far He simply adopts their views as current in His time in certain circles. His [Paul's] Eschatology is thus simple and self-consistent. He expects a Judgment, which at the appearing of the Son-of-Man Messiah will include the Angels as well as all generations of men."[45] Judgment is conceived of before the general resurrection.

The difference in these two eschatologies stems basically from a difference in opinion as to when the resurrection will occur. In the Apocalypses of Baruch and Ezra, the authors placed the resurrection at the end of the messianic kingdom. Jesus concurs with the Book of Daniel by placing the resurrection at the onset of the messianic kingdom. The scribes followed the teachings of the Apocalypses of Baruch and Ezra, which tied together the prophetic as well as the Danielic threads, linking them in a harmonious system. Since Paul was in agreement with the end as seen by the Apocalypses of Baruch and Ezra, it is reasonable to assume that these were the accepted views on which he was nurtured.

Schweitzer conceives an entire sequence of events which constitutes the end in accordance with the twofold eschatology of the scribes, culminating in death being destroyed at the end of the messianic kingdom. Further, Schweitzer maintains that judgment and resurrection can happen only at the end of the messianic kingdom. The kingdom, according to Paul, then exists only for those believers living when it finally breaks in upon the world.

There are, then, the two forms of blessedness, one belonging to the messianic and the other to the eternal. This leaves only those who have not died the pleasures of both forms of blessedness. However, those who have died and believed then shall participate in the eternal blessedness. "The eschatology of Paul is therefore quite different from that of Jesus, a fact which has been hitherto never duly appreciated. Instead of thinking as Jesus did along the lines of the simple eschatology of the Books of Daniel and Enoch, he represents the two-fold eschatology of the Scribes."[46]

However, it is not simply a matter of Paul's taking over these two eschatologies en masse, for to them he adds his characteristic thought.

In assuming that the Elect in the Messianic Kingdom possess the resurrection mode of existence, Paul is not asserting something more or less self-evident, but something *extraordinary,* something at variance with the character of his eschatology. This has not heretofore been sufficiently realised. Jesus assumes a resurrection to participation in the Messianic Kingdom, and this assumption is also held in the Johannine Apocalypse (Rev. 20:4-6): it therefore would have seemed quite natural that Paul should hold the same view.[47]

When the death of individuals within the church did occur, Paul rested in the thought that the resurrection took place only after the messianic kingdom. Thus, it was only consistent with his thought that all the dead must pass through the messianic kingdom and await the resurrection at its end. This problem was not foreseen by those who conceived of the traditional eschatology, for with the Messiah would come the fullness of the kingdom. It was only after the advent of Jesus, the Messiah, that they could fully realize that the Messiah had come without the completeness of the kingdom. Here it must be realized that we have only the Christians in mind; the Jews still continue to await the Messiah, at least in theory if not in fact.

These difficulties would have been readily resolved if Christ had returned within the life span of Paul, but of course he did not. Paul walked lightly around this difficulty by making the case that those who had died before the messianic kingdom would not have to wait through it until the final resurrection. He raises the possibility that there would be an earlier special resurrection so that these dead might become participants in both blessings and as such would not miss any of the glory. This ended the thought of the privilege of living on until the Messiah returned (1 Thess. 4:13-18). It is apparent that Paul himself had some difficulty understanding completely the meaning of death in the early church since he explains death in the Corinthian church as God's punishment for those who were not worthy of the Lord's Supper (1 Cor. 11:29-32).

In Hebrew thought it was believed that only those who were alive at the end were able to participate in the resurrection. Since the Hebrews did not view religion as being either personal or individual, their main concern was that they would see the continuity of the race, Israel. Therefore, it is not surprising that among Jewish circles there still continued the belief that only the survivors would participate in the resurrection (1 Cor. 15:12-18, 29-33). Schweitzer maintains that a core of such people resulted in the problem created by the church in Corinth. Yet it would appear that these same deniers of the resurrection had no difficulty in accepting the resurrection of Jesus—only of themselves. This is clearly seen as Paul argues from the specific resurrection to the general resurrection.

Dr. Schweitzer makes a case for the fact that the difficulty in the church at Corinth was the result of an ultraconservative group.[48] This could hardly be the case. It was far more difficult, and it was anything but ultraconservatism that flanked Paul.

Here Schweitzer attempts to make a simple solution to a far more complex problem. In response to these remarks W. D. Davies said:

> In view of what we have written above, Paul's eschatology is far simpler than Schweitzer would have us believe. It contains no reference to a Messianic Kingdom such as is contemplated in Baruch, 4 Ezra, and Revelation and can be briefly summarized as the early expectation of the Parousia when there would be a final judgement, a general resurrection of the righteous dead (and possibly of all the dead), the transformation of the righteous living and ensuing upon all this the final consummation, the perfected Kingdom of God when God would be all in all. It will be readily admitted that this interpretation of Paul's eschatology brings the Resurrection of Jesus into closer proximity to the final consummation than does the schema of Schweitzer. Within the latter the Resurrection of Jesus can hardly be said to occupy anything but a minor place; the consummation is very far removed from the Resurrection of Jesus because there intervenes between the two events the Messianic Kingdom.[49]

The specific solution of the churches is not known to us per se. It must have been somehow resolved by the churches or they would easily have gone under. The solution bore hard upon them and they must have, like Paul, accepted that the dead would arise with the advent of Christ. This obstacle may have been less than we have imagined since the Jewish Christians had come to a belief in the resurrection before Christ's death, and they trusted, with no proof, that God had drawn Abraham, Isaac, and Jacob to himself. Paul resolved this by the impartiality of the two resurrection theories. However much we may say for or against these theories of the resurrection, they must ultimately rest on Paul as the creator and innovator. There is no precedent for them. Previous Jewish eschatologies maintained that there would be one and only one resurrection, the difference being the timing. "When he decides to put upon the old garment of the two-fold eschatology of the Scribes the new patch of the resurrection-and-transformation concept, he does this under the influence not of the teaching of Jesus but of the fact of His death and resurrection. This is evident from the way that in 1st Thessalonians he deduces the resurrection of those who have died in Christ from the resurrection of Jesus."[50]

The mere presence of Jesus in the world must call for a change in classical eschatology. Plans and systems must be reworked to make them applicable to the new evidence. Perhaps Paul's weakness is a direct result of his attempt to be all inclusive in binding the old threads together. His greatest difficulty is that of the natural man and the new man having the same position until the final resurrection. It is surprising that emotion seems to have reached Paul before the wave of logic. On the one hand, it could be assumed that their fates, though different, could be similar to their prenatal existence. On the other, if a person was truly "asleep," which Paul maintains, there would be no difficulty since he would be quite unaware. There is also an internal inconsistency in that death is not defeated until the very end, yet Paul maintains that it has been completely abolished. This conflicts with his thought that only the "sting" had been removed. Also there is difficulty with the belief that those who live are immediately transformed into a mode of resurrection existence. Does not one have to die before he can attain this mode? This problem was latent in the teaching of Jesus and also acknowledged by the scribes.

The Apocalypse of Ezra, by maintaining that at the appearance of the kingdom all die together and pass into eternal life, answered this difficulty. The problem was inescapable. As Jesus had passed through the gates of death to take on the resurrection existence, so too would all the followers. This does not really seem to be a very large problem since the actual form is beyond our comprehension and would no longer appear to be a major obstacle.

Paul's conception is, that believers in mysterious fashion share the dying and rising again of Christ, and in this way are swept away out of their ordinary mode of existence, and form a special category of humanity. When the Messianic Kingdom dawns, those of them who are still in life are not natural men like others, but men who have in some way passed through death and resurrection along with Christ, and are thus capable of becoming partakers of the resurrection mode of existence, while other men pass under the dominion of death. And similarly, those who have died in Christ are not dead as others are, but have become capable through their dying and rising again with Christ or rising before other men.[51]

It would be a serious mistake for Paul or any other Christian to maintain that a being "in Christ" did not die. There does not seem to be any promise of the complete defeat of death until the end. Until that time all mankind, both Christians and "natural" men, are under its sway and as such must inevitably die. To assume that the death of the Christian, or of Christ for that matter, is any different from any other, is to fall into the same mistake with which the first Christians wrestled. The one thing that we can say with certainty is that Christ *died* and we must also die, for we are all natural men to that extent.

One cannot approach the subject of Pauline eschatology by assuming that what was apparent to Jesus was also apparent to Paul. While a large amount, it is true, is held in common, there are also wide differences. In the last analysis they must both be reconciled in the context of the whole of Christianity. The man who begins to think out the resurrection and its implications consistently and continually, will come across some profound thoughts and perhaps be labeled a mystic. If one places this at the front of his thoughts, he will be intensely changed. But how then, after the resurrection, does man stand in relation to his universe? Is he still a part of the natural world or has he indeed passed on to the world of the supernatural? If Jesus did enter into history as the Messiah, then we live in the post-messianic age and there is no longer a clear distinction between the Then and the Now, nor are past, present, and future such distinct, separate entities.

If Jesus has risen, that means, for those who dare to think consistently, that it is now already the supernatural age. And this is Paul's point of view. He cannot regard the resurrection of Jesus as an isolated event, but must regard it as the initial event of the rising of the dead in general. According to his view Jesus rose as "The First-fruits of those that had fallen asleep" (*aparche ton kekoimemenon,* I Cor. 15:20). We are therefore in the Resurrection period, even though the resurrection of others is still to come. Paul draws the logical inference from the fact that Jesus, after His earthly existence, was not simply rapt away to heaven in order to return thence in glory as the Messiah, but Himself passed through death and resurrection.[52]

Within the resurrection of Jesus, Paul came to see the beginning of the end, for the powers of the kingdom were operative in this world. After the firstfruits have been reaped, the other plants continue to grow and spread so that the full harvest will follow. Although one has to admire Schweitzer's statement, he must also be aware that it comes much closer to the truth and in so doing it violates the whole schematical position that Schweitzer has so laboriously written. Schweitzer, however, remains oblivious to this difficulty. Not only is this the essential truth of the Christian faith but it must be seen that this would in effect change our lives in every aspect and detail if we would live with Schweitzer's suggestion about the resurrection.

Of all the followers of Christ, no one has been able to think through the application of the resurrection to his life more intently and compatibly than Paul. It was Paul alone who gave proper respect to the resurrection. And hence it follows that he would also be the one to maintain that the traditional eschatology of old could no longer exist unchanged, but rather it must face up to the fact that all things now are completely different. This could be realized only by those who had steadied their eyes on the resurrection.

The continuing fellowship of the elect with their Messiah and with one another gives rise in due course to a Christ-mysticism which extended into the world. This is not the invention or innovation of Paul; the rudiments of it will be found in the teaching and preaching of Jesus. For as individuals the elect are bound together and to their Lord in an entirely new relationship of intense depth. Through this relationship of their corporal existence they have become as one through the death and resurrection of Jesus. Thus, for them the process of dying and rising has already begun even though there can be no external manifestation of this communion.

100

The content and the actions of Jesus are not simply limited to this world but must be thought out in the context of their cosmic significance. Thus, Paul finds in his doctrine of redemption with its ramifications that the angelic forces are being destroyed and that there is continual, although gradual, transformation of this worldly existence to a super-earthly existence. "The Pauline Mysticism is therefore nothing else than the doctrine of the making manifest, in consequence of the death and resurrection of Jesus, of the pre-existent Church (the Community of God)."[53]

From this concept there grew a solidarity among the believers that entered into this relationship in any depth. "The Spirit of Him that raised Jesus from the dead, which dwells in them, will also give life to their mortal bodies (Rom. 8:11). Being grafted into Christ's death, they are also grafted into His resurrection (Rom. 6:5) and have the certainty that they will live with Him (Rom. 6:8)."[54] The term *being in Christ* was as near as the believers could come to an expression of the very subjective experience this held for them. As one being is grafted into this relationship, the old individual subsides and the new being is left. One continues only as a small part of a larger body, and as such has to act in accordance with the desires and the will of the individuals who function beside him.

"The fact that the believer's whole being, down to his most ordinary everyday thoughts and actions, is thus brought within the sphere of the mystical experience has its effect of giving to this mysticism a breadth, a permanence, a practicability, and a strength almost unexampled elsewhere in mysticism. Certainly in this it is entirely different in character from the Hellenistic mysticism, which allowed daily life to go its own way apart from the mystical experience and without relation to it."[55] Mysticism must always be an intensely personal relation which defies complete defining of itself; the manifestation of such must, however, define itself through the media of human personality. We will always be at a loss when we come to Pauline mysticism and the foundations for it since the complete exposition of it by Paul has never been found.

The full understanding of what Paul meant by a "being-in-

Christ" is never systematically produced, and thus we are left with the implications which are stated in such a matter-of-fact way that they would appear self-evident. It would seem that the essence of Pauline mysticism was certainly not the most important thing to Paul, or he would have developed it for his followers. It is rather a case of each individual's working out his own salvation with fear and trembling and in such a manner that he will enter into his own relationship as a "being-in-Christ." There is no plan or scheme left for us to imitate or to develop rigidly which works to the advantage of the church. It is also apparent that those who so desired to find the meaning of Christian mysticism throughout the centuries had no difficulty in doing so if they were willing to give themselves over to it completely.

As one approaches the whole of apostolic writings, he is caught in a dilemma. On the one hand, he has horrible predictions of doom and, on the other hand, the mercy and love of God, which seem to far surpass our fondest desires. There are here two factors that seem so irreconcilable that they have resulted in driving many seekers away from the church. This, then, was something of the nature of the apostolic eschatology as it sought to deal with these difficulties and to bring them into the whole body of Christian thought. There was within Paul the growing belief that the works of God extend to all men because in God's sight all men are the same.

Again there was the dark and seamy side of the New Testament message which is "chiefly expressed in those passages which speak of the state of spiritual 'death' that awaits the children of this world. It is in the light of these utterances that we must interpret such words as 'perdition' ($\dot{a}\pi\omega\lambda\epsilon\dot{\iota}a$), and 'corruption' or 'decay' ($\phi\theta o\rho\dot{a}$), and 'destruction' ($\ddot{o}\lambda\epsilon\theta\rho os$). The state of being lost, of decay, and of destruction, is equivalent to that mysterious condition of death which is declared to be the appointed lot of sinners beyond the Judgement."[56]

Although the writings of John see death as a part of the present world, Paul usually thinks in terms of death as being part of the hereafter and the fate that shall be determined then.

In Romans (6:23) Paul said: "The wages of sin is death, but the free gift of God is eternal life in Christ Jesus our Lord."

It is frustrating and shattering to study the negative side of Paul's doctrine. Paul had a fascination for death which was like an obsession. His concept of death was twofold in that he saw it as both a physical entity and a spiritual state or existence.

His references to it are so frequent, and exceed so much in variety of meaning all contemporary example, as to suggest a personal characteristic. He has recourse to the symbolism of "death" whenever he is deeply moved by the sad and stern aspect of things, and whenever he wishes to describe painful experiences or any want of sensibility. Sometimes he uses it in an extremely rhetorical way, as when he said, "I die daily"; "death worketh in us, but life in you"; "if Christ be in you, the body is dead." Again this phraseology often indicates the idea that those who are under sway of any one influence are free from the power of the opposite, as in the declaration that those who are alive to God are dead to sin. In this aspect, the symbol of death and dying is devoid of all colour of its own and takes a bright or a dark meaning according to the connection in which it occurs.[57]

Paul likens baptism to burial in that for the Christian it is his crucifixion and as such the believers can be considered dead. "An excellent example also, of the hyperbolical way in which he speaks of 'dying' is found in the statement, 'sin revived, and I died.' Clearly, it was not the habit of the Apostle to weigh his terms with care, or to measure his language in a scientific spirit; and he employed the tremendous symbolism of death in cases where writers of a different temperament would have expressed themselves with more moderation and variety. And he thus lays himself open to the danger of being misunderstood by literal and laborious minds. We may conjecture that he never expected his words to be so carefully examined, and would have been surprised at the importance which has often been attached to his impetuous expressions."[58]

One, however, dare not take the meaning of Paul's words lightly. His prophecy "the wages of sin is death" is as profound as it is contemporary. To Paul and his tradition there was nothing more appalling than physical dissolution. This he approached with utter conviction and sincerity and gave his life over so that others might see these implications and ramifications. "He saw in the king of terrors a fitting symbol of the uttermost spiritual doom. For him, as for Philo, to be unspiritual was to be dead now, and was to be moving towards a climax of death beyond the grave. To fail of eternal life at the last was to be given over to the powers of ruin and decay."[59]

When we turn to the negative side of Paul's message, we see that the concepts of Gehenna and its torments are conspicuous by their absence. We know that Paul was nurtured in rabbinic thought, which was continually upholding the symbols of eternal fire. Yet, here he is silent. Nothing could be more profound than this. In doing this he sets himself over against Judaism, the Synoptic tradition, and the teachings of Jesus. Could it be that Paul was really closer to the truth than we have believed? It must be at once apparent that he could not endorse or promote the concept of perpetual torment which Jesus had supported. In all his letters there is only one place where Paul even attempts to suggest this conception (Rom. 2:8-11). It is far more common for him to speak in terms of death, decay, and perdition than destruction by perpetual fires.

Although Paul went out of his way to tie in all the existing forms of eschatology, he clearly rejected the symbol of Gehenna as being unsuited for his beliefs or his teachings. Yet there is the possibility that what he raised may have been far worse; then there was no need to call on the superficial concepts of Gehenna to invoke belief by fear. Paul believed that the most tragic event that could confront an individual is that he might *die* after he was *dead*. This means that as individuals we would be given over to irrevocable death rather than the converse of eternal life. This indeed was much more to be feared than anything we might imagine.

We might be ready to say that the prophecy, "If ye live after the flesh, ye must die," pointed to a fixed and final event, if we did not remember the similar and clearly imaginative saying, "Sin revived, and I died." We have always to bear in mind that the terms of the "death" imagery had no such theological content for him as they have for us, to whom they represent a long dogmatic tradition. He had been nurtured in the Jewish Church which had no assured doctrine of immortality, far less of ultimate destiny; and members of that Church had spoken of death as the wages of sin, without themselves having any faith in a life to come. Also, St. Paul was a pupil of a Rabbinic school which was only beginning to consider the problems of future existence. Hence, words like "death" and "perdition" were for him still in a plastic state, and were ready to take many different forms of meaning under the touch of his individual and creative genius.[60]

The first occasion when Paul addressed himself to these details at any length occurred in the letter to the Corinthians, in which he "exhibits with wonderful completeness all the varied characteristics of the Apostle's genius; his impetuous logic, his rhetoric, his indignation and pathos, the electric leap of his thought from point to point, his passionate faith and hope. It is also a signal illustration of that originality of mind which enabled him to employ the old apocalyptic forms in such a way as to express through them his own distinctive gospel and to make them the instrument of his speculative thought."[61] It is within this context that Paul's true uniqueness shows through, and it is against this that we must examine any doubts and scepticisms concerning his authority and apostleship. It is in this manner that his apostleship *par excellence* shows through, and this is precisely why so many people think Paul stands far above his colleagues "in Christ."

There are only two sayings of little importance in the whole Pauline corpus that reflect the traditional doom of the New Testament. But these are sufficient to indicate that it was a matter both serious and present because within these there is the thought of perdition and exclusion from the kingdom. Paul believed that unregenerate men were already "dead" in this world and as such were under the bondage of "decay" and "perdition," but there was always the strong element of hope that they might arouse themselves to an awareness and change their state before it became too late. The question arises, When does this hope end? This we are not told. Can one maintain that those who are under the bondage of decay and death are in an endless and incurable state forever? Conversely, there are no specific grounds on which to argue that man can have salvation even after his death. The ambiguity of this situation has left room for the followers to hold up Paul as the disciple of universal salvation. "The most forcible objections to the Universalist view are that the Apostle's warnings of approaching doom do have a note of finality in them and that his prophecies of a final reconciliation do not certainly imply that every man will enjoy the fulness of redemption."[62]

While it is basically true that Paul held mostly to the concepts of the Jewish fathers, after his confrontation with the Christ his faith in the redeeming love of Christ transcended all other thoughts, and personal beliefs had to give way. This became such a shining light in his life that it truly blinded him to the irrelevant difficulties that at first disturbed him and the churches with which he came into contact. "Till the last he spoke of those who were lost, whose end was perdition, but he became less and less able to set limit or bound to the reconciling energy of God in Jesus Christ the Lord. All this is clear; but beyond this we cannot go. We do not know that he ever held one definite, coherent theory as to the final state of mankind, or that on this subject he had 'beat his music out,' and completed the development of his thought."[63] If this is true, then it is up to the followers to work out the notes until the song is completed.

There is no greater difficulty in dealing with Paul than approaching his words with the assumption that they have the same meaning and relevance for us today as they had for Paul. Not only are we separated in thought but the proximity of the resurrection shaded his entire thought and approach, which we can by no means duplicate.

To the Greeks that he encountered, death came also like the darkness of a cloud over their shining lives. The epitaphs on their sepulchers bear witness to this; they use such words as *bitter, ruinous,* and *relentless.* Nevertheless, euphemisms were far more uncommon to the Greeks than they are to our enlightened age. The underworld stretched before them like an inevitable abyss which they must enter to exist in a "withered" form.

As for the Hebrew, he believed in God, whose first claim was that he was a living God. Somewhere along the way—it is exceedingly difficult to set the exact time—the Hebrews came to believe that there was a connection between sin and death. By the time of Paul this lay on the consciousness of the populace. They believed that sin not only resulted in personal catastrophe but could and did affect families even into the third generation. Although these roots are hopelessly obscured, this belief followed logically from a sophisticated view of sin. Sin is that element that separates man from God. Therefore, death also separates man from God—in a fuller and more ultimate manner.

If death continued to hold the upper hand, it was both judgment and doom. Thus, it was not hard for Hebrews to believe that sin and death were inextricably interwoven. In the Book of Ezekiel we read, "The soul that sins shall die." This probably is the same belief that underlies the writing of the third chapter of Genesis. But even for the most primitive tribesman there is something about death that offends. Death seems to be unnatural, but immortality seems to be the normal course.

The frailty and transiency of which it is the crowning proof, the sharp pangs which accompany its approach, the unsightliness and decay which follow its presence, the bitter pain of soul it inflicts on those who are left behind—all these, its associations impress them as an outrage upon a creation made in the image of God. Plainly, therefore, we may say that for the Hebrew mind the physical fact has a spiritual significance. . . . Thus death is only intelligible to them in the light of the weakness and sinfulness of humanity.[64]

So we see that the background for death is the fearful separation from God. Death then pronounces the last word on man's fate and destiny and therefore always speaks of doom. To Paul's mind there could be no more grievous penalty for sin than death—the death which would mean banishment from God and the complete paralysis of the individual.

The Hebrew filled his mind with the fulfillment of life. He

looked for pleasure in having a large family, prosperity, communion with God, and a long life. This was how to live out one's destiny in the fullest and best tradition. And to a certain extent he must have shrunk back from a gloomy and shadowy existence in Sheol, which was despairing and hopeless. Death would have meant to Paul utter separation from God, which would be overwhelmingly experienced and would eventually rend a person asunder. Death was chaos, ruin, and disaster. Whatever we come to understand as Pauline doctrine in eschatology, it will be impossible to make any clear demarcation between Paul's historical tradition and his personal encounter.

The clue to understanding Paul's eschatology is in the expression, "I have been crucified with Christ." What made all the difference in Paul's life and thought was this same risen Lord who appeared to him on the Damascus journey and had been crucified for his own personal sin. For in that meeting Paul found acceptance beyond himself, acceptance that he could not fathom, only acknowledge. Thus, sin became for Paul what it had become for Christ. Christ died for Paul, and Paul must now live for Christ. This is the fullest meaning of having been "crucified with Christ." Professor Denney ably states the case: "The faith which abandons itself to Christ is at the same time a receiving of the Spirit of Christ, or of what to experience is the same thing, Christ in the Spirit; there are not two things here but one, though it can be represented in the two relations which the words Faith and Spirit suggest."[65]

Baptism became both the sign and the symbol of this new faith. It very vividly portrays the old man going down to the bottom never to be seen again, as the new man rises fresh and purified by the water. This is an appropriate symbol of the atoning death and resurrection as the individual passes from this sinful life in the flesh, cancelled by the cross, and rises anew with the risen Lord to the completeness and fullness of the life in the Spirit. "But obviously, the picture also symbolises the relation of the believer to the Spirit. For all that has happened to him in the experience of salvation, his death to sin (immersion beneath the water), and his entrance upon a new life (emergence from the water), is really accomplished for him in response to his faith, accomplished by the Divine operation; is the work, as St. Paul would put it, of the Holy Spirit."[66]

Most of this chapter has dealt with a topical approach to the problems of Pauline eschatology. This seemed to be the most reasonable way to enter upon the discussion because Paul makes no attempt to present his eschatology in a systematic framework. The framework must be superimposed, and this has been attempted. Now, for completeness' sake it will be necessary to turn to a chronological survey to determine the development of thought in its evolutionary form. Since the dating of these books is not completely settled, the form that will be followed will be that of Professor James Denney because he gives the most thorough and complete exposition of these epistles in regard to the problem of death. The order is as follows: Thessalonians, Corinthians, Galatians, Romans, and the letters of the imprisonment—Colossians, Ephesians, and Philippians.

First and Second Thessalonians

In the first letter Paul eagerly expects Jesus' early return. As certainly as Jesus died and rose again, he will return and take with him those that have fallen asleep. Within these writings the Parousia, resurrection, and final judgment are closely connected as parts of one supreme event. There is here no introduction of a millennial reign on earth. When Jesus descends, the dead in Christ shall rise so that the living and the resurrected righteous will be caught up to meet the Lord in the air and will be forever with him (1 Thess. 4:16-18). The reference is only to Christians since there is no indication that there will be any resurrection of the wicked. By implication one can conclude that after the resurrection of the righteous of the world, those who did not share will remain in destruction. This is the concept of "vengeance" referred to in 2 Thessalonians 1:8.

The end will come about by the direct intervention of God when evil has reached its apex. This is in direct agreement with Jewish apocalyptic thought. This day of the Lord cannot come "unless the rebellion [ἡ ἀποστασία] comes first, and the man of lawlessness is revealed, the son of perdition, . . . [whose]

coming [is] by the activity of Satan . . . and with all wicked deception for those who are to perish" (2 Thess. 2:3, 9, 10). It is the power of evil that shall call this into being by its strength. At this time Christ will descend from heaven and "slay [Satan] with the breath of his mouth" (2 Thess. 2:8).

This is all to occur within Paul's own lifetime (1 Thess. 2: 19). Obvious signs will precede the actual event (2 Thess. 2). The appearance will be that of a thief in the night bringing with him the day of judgment. Those who have died in Christ are to sleep on until the resurrection.

Professor Denney thinks the only indisputable, relevant passage in these letters is 1 Thessalonians 5:9-10: "God has not destined us for wrath, but to obtain salvation through our Lord Jesus Christ, who died for us so that whether we wake or sleep we might live with him." In reply to the question, What did Christ do for us with regard to salvation? Paul would say simply that he died for us. He died for us because this was the price that sin exacted.

In the nature of things the relation of sin and death made it binding on Him to die if He was to annul sin. . . . [This passage] suggests that His power to redeem is dependent on His making all our experiences His own. If we are to be His in death and life, then He must take our death and life to Himself. If what is His is to become ours, it is only on the condition that what is ours He first makes His. There is the same suggestion in Romans 14:9: "To this end Christ died, and lived again, that He might be Lord of both the dead and the living."[67]

It was only by opening himself fully to the whole gamut of human experience and expression that Jesus could truly become the Lord of all mankind. It was this willingness to stand with us, or even more to stand for us, that represented the love of God and the love of Christ against the powers of evil. It was only by Christ's stooping to the utter depths of sinful humanity that he could do us any good. But first and foremost "Christ died for our sins."

It was the awareness of the revelation begun in the resurrection of Christ that instantaneously called forth the hope for the fulfillment of salvation for the second coming of Christ. When he does come, all will surrender dominion and power to God (1 Cor. 15:24-28). It is this anxious expectation that elicits the resurrection of Christ and his second coming in the same breath when Paul refers to the substance of the faith of those Gentiles who had accepted the gospel (1 Thess. 1:9-10). The radically new element in the lives of these members is Paul's unshaken hope that God will be all in all. When they were Gentiles, they had no knowledge of Christ and were thus considered as "having no hope and without God in the world" (Eph. 2:12). But Paul can now speak out of joy in telling them that their attitude toward the problem of death is no longer that of others "who have no hope" (1 Thess. 4:13). At this stage it is true that Paul believed that after death the soul would live on in the interim period. This is evident in his answer to the church at Thessalonica (1 Thess. 4:15-18).

First Corinthians

First Corinthians is without a doubt the *locus classicus* of the Christian faith with regard to eschatology. A great deal of thought is compactly placed in this one book and especially concentrated in the fifteenth chapter. In fact, there is so much content here that Karl Barth wrote a whole volume centered on this single chapter. It would be far too consuming an enterprise to discuss the book at length; however, it will be of interest to reiterate some of the details.

The letters were addressed specifically to meet the problems of the Corinthian church. Because Corinth was such a unique mixture of tradesmen and other people, it is not difficult to see how they got into so many wrangles. Some of these individuals may have attempted to interpret Christianity in terms of the Greek gods. Others may have been divided on social, economic, and theological differences. These differences may have been the means of rationalizing their own positions. But whatever we might conjecture, the fact remains that the church at Corinth was badly torn and perhaps was the most difficult of all the churches that Paul established.

Paul pleads that they turn away from their various and sundry ways.

"Wherefore, I beseech you, be ye followers of me" (4:16). The context makes this unmistakably clear: Come down from your wisdom, from your self-content, from your wealth, from the kingly consciousness which now fills you as Christians; come down from the brilliance of the all too Greek Christianity into which you have strayed, and, if you want to sail under the Pauline flag, come down into the foolishness and ignominy of Christ, where the truth is, where not man, not even the Christian man, but God is great, and where I, Paul, your father in Christ, am to be found.[68]

Barth continues that it is not proper that "the testimony of Christ should be made an object of religious athleticism and brilliance, as the Greek religious world was fond of doing, regarding in an all too human manner the Great, the Estimable, the Amazing simply in the relation of Either-Or."[69]

There is from God the Word of the cross (1:18), which is salvation and as such is God's Word for us. "So are things placed in the scales in the Cross of Christ, which is the focus of the testimony of Him; on the one side, death is the last, the absolute last which we can see and understand; on the other side is life, of which we know nothing at all, which we can only comprehend as the life of *God* Himself, without having in our hands anything more than an empty conception thereof—apart from the fullness that God alone gives and His revelation in the resurrection."[70]

In dealing with some rather irrelevant problems in the letter to the Corinthians, Paul tackles the greatest problem of all. This is the problem of death, which is only a small part of the problem of evil. This comes as the crown and apex of all Pauline thought and has endeared him to the Christian faith forever. While Paul formerly tended to scold, he now turns to the most positive assertion and apologia of the Christian church. For it is the resurrection of the dead that makes the whole of Christianity universally relevant to mankind. "The Resurrection of the Dead is the point from which Paul is speaking and to which he points. From this standpoint, not only the death of those now living, but, above all, their life *this side* of the threshold of death, is in the apostolic sermon, veritably seen, understood, judged, and placed in the light of the last severity, the last hope."[71]

Here, then, in this one chapter is the expression of Paul's doctrine of the last things. There is perhaps no profounder statement in Christian dogma than this. Karl Barth maintains that whether history is contracted or expanded, there is still the ultimate message. It was from the beginning the same as it will be at the consummation. It is the Word for all time, constant, unchanging, and immutable. It transcends all, for in itself it is the Infinite, the Alpha and Omega, and the clue to existence.

Whatever Paul may have lifted in those Corinthian hearts in the realm of faith, hope, and trust, all subsided in his absence and in the presence of the greater question of death. Perhaps the very background of this stems from the sheer materialism of Christianity. What does Christianity mean for me? What benefits shall I derive from it? This seems very crude, but the form is so common that one cannot escape it as a possibility. So Paul must begin with what he preached so strongly and succinctly, invoking the very core of their beliefs and confession, hoping that these familiar words will reach again their full significance. "To *follow* the movement of his thoughts from afar and to hear with more or less distinctness the most vital things which he intended to say and yet nowhere can say—all this we must now show. Let us be prepared for partial failure from the start. We are probably (and not only historically) too far away from Paul to be able to approach him here, even approximately."[72]

In all honesty it can be maintained that Paul is not here teaching new doctrine. The church is too torn and confused to begin with something new. This is his same thought delivered to the believers, meticulously worked out to convince and to reassure them. It makes no attempt to lead them to other pastures but rather attempts to bring the straying sheep back to the fold. "They merely took offence, as Lietzmann believes, at the Jewish doctrine of the resurrection, from the standpoint of the Greek belief in immortality, or as Bousset suggests: at the unconscious compromise between the Jewish and the Greek conception of the future life, within which Paul moved, but for the rest obviously did not dream of unravelling the antagonism between themselves and Paul in its fundamental acuteness."[73]

The meaning of 1 Corinthians 15:12-28 is that the resurrection of Jesus from the dead depends on the general resurrection for its validity. It is quite plain that we could say "he died" and "he was buried," but the action of God depends on the statement that he was raised from the dead. The first two incidents occurred quite naturally without the interference of anyone or anything; it was only when he was raised from the dead that it was necessary to look to an outside force. And if he was raised from the dead, then it was possible for him to be seen. After his appearances he moved on to encounters that transcended the normal concept of personal encounters. There is little known about these post-resurrection appearances, and it would thus appear that our lack of knowledge is as striking as the knowledge we have.

The real point that Paul is driving at is whether the church can exist when it no longer continues to believe in the resurrection, the ground and core of its existence. The absence of this belief leads to a purely illegitimate existence. The church from time to time must seriously ask itself, "What does this mean?" The church must continually endeavor to find new answers to this question and make them revelant for society. "Paul does not shrink from putting his 'Either-Or' so sharply that beside the impossible, unbelievable, inaccessible gospel of the Resurrection of the Dead there is left only the abyss of an utterly radical scepticism towards everything divine, even towards everything that is humanly highest, holding the danger that somebody may fall into it and be unable to get out."[74] Paul makes no attempt to delude himself or ourselves.

He does not defend himself, but he attacks: Christianity without resurrection, and says as forcibly as he can, that it is a lie and a deceit, not because it is still without this article of faith, but because it is in itself an illusion, a fiction. Whereas they regard Paul as a dogmatist, who loads their reason with an unnecessary, unrealizable idea, he shows them that they are those who (not with their doubts and negations, but with what they admit and presumably also *believe*) are playing blind-man's-buff with ideas divorced from the real actuality. In attempting to escape from the resurrection as the alleged absurd, they are making an absurdity of what to them appears *not* absurd, but reasonable and tolerable; they are sawing off the branch upon which they are sitting.[75]

There can be nothing more tragic than a religious body that has become so out of tune with the original sound waves that it no longer recognizes them and, indeed, attempts to rationalize their presence away. Then again, if the resurrection proceeds only on the basis that One proceeded from the dead and has no relevance for any followers, it dupes its followers to believe in a supernatural event which has no relevance for their individual lives and as such is not worthy enough to hold one's highest allegiance. If Christianity is sheer philosophy, ethics, or disciplined living—then let it be that but do not interject the concepts of the miraculous and supernatural being in order to bolster up an idealism. Followers should then turn away from the resurrection and its demands on, and applications to, their daily existence. Thus, one can embrace Jesus as the supreme teacher of righteousness, the leader and example for the good moral and ethical life. Paul obviously had put the emphasis of his whole teaching and preaching on the wrong phases of the Christian life. Was the apostle wrong in his emphasis? Obviously those that opposed him so vehemently at Corinth returned to the membership and multiplied.

Paul would maintain that death and judgment rule also on this side of life.

Or whence comes the desire to know anything else? Whence do we lay claim to the arrogance that dying means redemption? Dying is pitilessly nothing but dying, only the expression of the corruptibility of all finite things, if there be no *end* of the finite, no *perishing* of the corruptible, no *death* of death. We are not, with edifying enthusiasm, to just try and push past the fact of death, but to be right sober at the last (verse 34), just as in front of the Cross of Christ, and say to ourselves, that this last word attainable by us: that we must *die*, gives, at any rate, no occasion for religious optimism regarding our situation as understood apart from revelation.[76]

The basic error of the Corinthians was much the same one that confronts the modern church. It was not that they denied the resurrection of Christ. They accepted it as an act of God once and for all, but this was precisely where they failed. For their life in Christ ended with resurrection rather than beginning there. They gave up just where they should have started. It was the finished work, full and complete. It was carried no farther. They did not see it as the example, standard, or norm of their own personal lives. "They comprehended what had happened in Christ in the world as something finished and satisfying in itself. In reality it is only a beginning, in fact only an indication; Christ is come to deliver the Kingdom to the Father, after He has taken their force away from the powers warring against God, and has undermined the world, so to speak (Zündel) (verse 24). The hostile powers are all independent beginnings and forces, whose relationship to God is not yet clear. We must see Christ in *conflict* with all that is in this sense obscure, not at peace with it."[77]

Paul raises the problem of being baptized for the dead, which seems to be as mysterious as it is esoteric. Although it may always be open for speculation, there is not a great deal that can be said accurately about it. Professor Barth states that "verse 29 is a *crux interpretum,* and the reader must make up his mind that even I cannot tell him much that is satisfying on this point. What is the meaning of 'which are baptized for the dead'? To be really baptized again for others who are already dead, to be baptized vicariously for them?"[78]

Indeed, the life of the apostle had a special meaning in that before the face of death he acknowledged life. "In defiance of death, and thus in face of death, there where nothing but death is to be perpetually reckoned with, or in that case with the resurrection itself, with the end, or in that case with the entire new beginning itself, but not with that which lies between, only from thence. If this Thence be removed, the apostleship becomes a stupid farce. It would then be really appropriate to discuss the requirements and possibilities of life (of life apart from the Cross) in a somewhat more practical manner."[79]

Barth continues: "That I [Paul], as apostle, can only reckon with death, or then with the resurrection itself, that alone places you in the position, with apparent rightness without fear of death, without faith in resurrection, to regard it differently. But how could I persist in this Either-Or if I were not sure of my cause? if I did not know that the oppression of death must be for the sake of the Life which I preach, which can only be preached from just this standpoint?"[80] Perhaps it was not strictly a matter of some people accepting the resurrection and others denying it, but rather of a continuum with all shades of belief and disbelief. Doubtless few have seen the resurrection with the depth, consistency, and intensity that Paul did; consequently, there have been few that could agree with him completely.

Bodily existence does not continue in flesh and blood since there is virtually no purpose for this body to continue in the limits and confines of earthly existence. In reality it has nothing to do with flesh and blood. Paul came to see that beyond death the body was a constricting factor for it gave entry to the true depth and expression of human personality. At death God steps in to redeem us even though we are unredeemable.

The corruptibility, dishonour, and weakness of man is, in fact, that of his *corporeality*. Death is the death of his body. If death be not only the end—but the turning point, then the new life must consist in the repredication of his corporeality. To be sown and to rise again must then apply to the *body*. The body is man, body in relation to a non-bodily, determined, indeed, by this non-bodily, but body. The change in the relationship of the body to this non-bodily is just the resurrection. Not, therefore, some transition of man to merely non-bodily existence. Of such Paul knows nothing whatever. The persisting subject is rather just the body. It is "natural" body this side, "spiritual" body beyond the resurrection.[81]

As far as doctrinal changes or insights are concerned, the following observations can be made. Basically, 1 Corinthians is very similar to Thessalonians. The Parousia and the final judgment are to occur within the apostle's lifetime. They are to be preceded by severe trials which will last only for a short period. The judgment will follow immediately after the Parousia; there will be no lapse of time. Christ will be the Judge, and people will be judged by works. The individual's resurrection is organically connected to the resurrection of Christ. This is limited to the righteous, who will retain some personal bodily qualities. In the new form there are to be continuity and discontinuity, but nevertheless contingent on each other.[82] The faithless are to remain naked or to have no existence at all.

The resurrection of the faithful will follow immediately after death and will not be put off until the Parousia since there is no waiting for the trumpet. "Of this variance between his living and growing thought and inherited Jewish views the Apostle does not seem conscious in I Corinthians. In the 2nd Epistle to the Corinthians we shall find that the Apostle has become conscious of the inherent inconsistencies of his former view, which was the traditional one, and abandoned it in favour of the doctrine of a resurrection of the righteous following immediately on death."[83] Paul's teaching here is not entirely novel but readily follows the more advanced apocalyptic literature.

Christ's kingdom will end with the conclusion of this world. Because the resurrection is only for those who continue in a vital, dynamic relationship with Christ, there is no resurrection for the wicked. Nothing per se is said about the doom of the wicked, except general statements that all will be judged according to their works (2 Cor. 5:10).

There is also a word about grace here, for we were all bought with a price (1 Cor. 6:20; 7:23). Grace is freely given and freely received, yet this is not in the least to infer that it is cheap. One should glorify God for such an expensive price and beware of becoming servants of man. Our responsibility is to God.

While one is hard pressed to make any elaboration out of this divine economics, it is quite clear that the work of man's salvation was a costly work, and that the cost, however we are to construe it, is represented by the death of Christ. Salvation cannot be taken for granted as a small and unimportant thing; it is, rather, the enormous cosmic struggle. "Salvation *is* a difficult thing, an incredible thing, an impossible thing; it is the miracle of miracles that such a thing should be; the wonder of it never ceases, and it nowhere finds a more thrilling expression than in Paul's words, 'Ye were bought with a price.' "[84]

Second Corinthians

Paul begins defensively about his position as an apostle. No doubt he was under attack and he used this opportunity to make known his position to his opponents, who were probably not Corinthians. There are two bases for his assertions; one is his comprehension of the doctrine of Christ and the other is his latter-day success in preaching it. Not only did he present the gospel but he indeed bore about in his body the dying of Jesus. Here it is clear that, for Paul, to preach Christ was to do so at the expense of his life. The trials and tribulations of his discipleship would eventually cost him his life, for daily he feels the force of death overtaking him (1:5; 4:10).

In the fifth chapter is the exposition of what Christ's death was in relationship to sin.

The motive of his conduct was always the same. "The love of Christ constrains us," he writes, "because we thus judge, that one died for all (so then all died), and died for all that they who live should no longer live for themselves, but for Him who died for them, and rose again" (see verses 14 and 15). The importance of this passage is that it connects the two relations in which Paul is in the habit of defining Christ's death, that is its relation to the love in which it originated, and to the sin with which it dealt. It shows us also how to construe these two things in relation to each other. Christ's death, we are enabled to see, was a loving death so far as men are concerned only because in that death He took the responsibilities of men upon Himself. Deny that, and it will be impossible to show any ground on which the death can be construed as a loving death at all.[85]

Denney's theory behind this is:

It is that one died for all; ὑπὲρ πάντων means that the interest of all was aimed at and involved in the death of the one. How it was involved in it these words do not enable us to say. They do not by themselves show the connection between Christ's death and the world's good. But Paul draws an immediate inference from them: "so then all died." In one sense, it is irrelevant and interrupts his argument. He puts it into a hurried parenthesis, and then eagerly resumes what it had suspended. "One died for all (so then all died), and died for all that they who live should no longer live to themselves, but to Him who died for them and rose again." Yet it is in this immediate inference—that the death of Christ *for* all involved the death *of* all—that the missing link is found. It is because Christ's death has this inclusive character, because, as Athanasius puts it, "the death of all was fulfilled in the Lord's body", that His death has in it a power which puts constraint on men to live for Him.[86]

What, then, is the relationship of Christ's death to our own? What is in this that has the power to constrain men ever since these words were uttered?

And this is precisely what we discover in the inferential clause: "so then all died". This clause puts as plainly as it can be put the idea that His death was equivalent to the death of all. In other words, it was the death of all men which was died by Him. Were this not so, His death would be nothing to them. It is beside the mark to say that His death is died by them rather than theirs by Him. The very point of the apostle's argument may be said to be that in order that they may die His death He must first die theirs. Our dying His death is not, in the New Testament, a thing which we achieve on our own initiative or out of our own resources. It is the fruit of His dying ours. If it is our death that Christ died on the cross, there is in the cross the constraint of an infinite love. But if it is not our death at all, if it is not our burden and doom that He has taken to Himself there, what then is it to us? The death of all was died by Him. His death can put the constraint of love upon all men, only when it is thus judged.[87]

Therefore, reconciliation is the subject of this death. This was what God was doing in and through Christ—reconciling men to God. We see that the subject of this one great divine act is God and the object is man. It was always God who stooped to take the initiative and paid the overwhelming cost. *Katallassein* does not translate exactly into English; we assume that one has to lay aside all fear, distrust, and love of evil, and enter, in point of fact, into relations of peace and friendship with God. The work of reconciliation, in the sense of the New Testament, is a work which is finished, and which we must conceive to be finished before the gospel is preached. It is only with this concept that the church must and can move forward. "It is a work—as Cromwell said of the covenant—*outside of us,* in which God so deals in Christ with the sin of the world, that it shall no longer be a barrier between Himself and men . . . . Reconciliation in the New Testament sense, is not something which is being done; it is something which is done."[88] Unless it is a completed work, we have no real gospel for man. " . . . 'He died for our sins.' When the sinless one, in obedience to the will of the Father, died on the cross the death of all, the death in which sin had involved all, then, and in that sense, God made Him to be sin for all."[89]

Thus, if the reconciliation of man to God is the finished work, the only reconciliation that can remain is man's reconciliation to man. There is the call to participate in the extension of reconciliation by becoming a part of the reconciling community, the Christian church. It is in accepting Christ's death for us and continuing his work by dying unto him that we can become part of this community.

There are in this letter the following elements of change. There is tremendous growth—the time of the end has been expanded by Paul and the understanding of the kingdom has been deepened. The kingdom has to spread and will cause the culmination of evil. The world will thus be faced with the conversion of all mankind. The Parousia is followed by judgment that will be by works, which are the normal expression of faith. There is no form of retribution other than by man's works (11:15).

The resurrection is to follow immediately after the death of the individual. It would appear that Paul caught his own inconsistencies with regard to the placing of the resurrection. The main doctrine of Pauline eschatology is rethought and reshaped in the context of 2 Corinthians 5:1-8, which begins, "We know that if the earthly tent we live in is destroyed, we have a building from God, a house not made with hands, eternal in the heavens."

At first (v. 4) Paul expresses his deep desire to live on to the Parousia in order that he might escape dissolution and thus fulfill his highest hopes. However, in the much more realistic verses he squarely faces up to the possibilities of death. In regard to the prospect before the elect, their possible shape, Paul says that we come into the possession of an immortal body in heaven. It would be hoped that the elect receive their bodies at the point of their election, but as the text shows it is not until death. This new body is a combination of the divine gift of God and the works of the individual.

Paul changes his terminology, and instead of speaking of the resurrection of the righteous at the Parousia, he speaks of their revelation in glory. There is thus a spiritual resurrection of the faithful that continues. Then later Paul can say that they "have been brought from death to life" (Rom. 6:13), like those "raised with [Christ] through faith" (Col. 2:12; 3:1). God even "made us alive together with Christ . . . and raised us up with him, and made us sit with him in the heavenly places" (Eph. 2:5-6).

Galatians

The Letter of Paul to the Galatians deals more with the death of Christ than does any other book in the entire New Testament. It was Christ who gave himself for our sins so that he might redeem us. There are the strong words of Paul as he anathematizes those who preach another gospel. Then at the conclusion of chapter two, Paul states his unshaken conviction that Christianity is a new and true religion which is an end in itself and can never be compromised or complemented. This is because of the uniqueness and the power of the death of Christ.

"I have been crucified with Christ; it is no longer I who live, but Christ who lives in me; the life I now live in the flesh I live by faith in the Son of God, who loved me and gave himself for me" (2:20). "The whole of Christian life is a response to the love exhibited in the death of the Son of God for men."[90] Total trust is the only right response for man when confronted

122

with the living Christ. To add or subtract from this is compromise.

If righteousness is by law, as he sums it up in one of his passionate and decisive words, then Christ died for nothing (2:21). Paul knew by experience that all he was, or could ever become as a Christian, came out of the cross. . . . "God forbid that I should glory, save in the cross of our Lord Jesus Christ, whereby the world is crucified unto me and I unto the world" (Gal. 6:14 A.V. mg.). . . . We may say that the aim of the Epistle to the Galatians is to show that all Christianity is contained in the cross, which is the generative principle of everything Christian in the life of man.[91]

The law falls to the background; it is all the cross.

Paul worked out his religion between himself and his Creator. For Christ came and lived under the Law and was subject to the Law. This not only was part of his humanity but was the element that led to his death and crucifixion. However, Christ came to break us from the spell of the Law through his obedience (Gal. 3:13). For Paul the whole subject of Christ's death is known only through obedience. This is the key to the mystery of Christ's death. Now we are no longer subject to the Law, but through Christ's obedience we are now subject to him. "Death is the curse of the law. It is the experience in which the final repulsion of evil by God is decisively expressed; and Christ died. In His death everything was made His that sin had made ours—everything in sin except its sinfulness. There is no *essential* significance in the crucifixion, as though it would have been impossible to say that Christ became a curse for us if He had died in any other way. The curse, in truth, is only one of Paul's synonyms for the death of Christ—one which is relative, no doubt, to the conception of Christ as 'under the law', but which for its meaning is entirely independent of the passage in Deuteronomy."[92]

Those who have been crucified with Christ have died to the passions and lusts of the flesh. Those who have pried open the mystery of Calvary and now live with Christ are aware that sin is sentenced to doom (5:24). To come to any depth of relationship with its meaning is truly the end of our fleshly existence. To this continuing thought Paul thus turns in conclusion: "Far be it from me to glory except in the cross of our Lord Jesus Christ, by which the world has been crucified to me, and I to the world" (6:14). Paul runs full circle in this letter and thus ends precisely where he began.

Romans

The Letter of Paul to the Romans, coming a bit later and addressed more in summary than to a church that is torn, such as the Corinthian church, is not so controversial. The underlying theme is how shall such a sinful creature as man be made righteous in the sight of God. The righteousness of God is expressed through the death of Christ (3:25). So again we see, as in Galatians, that the death of Christ is the source of all Christian truth and meaning. It is the focus of all God's actions and love, and expounding or developing it is all of what is Christian theology. It negates the past, makes way for the future, and assures us in our day-to-day transitory existence as we move on to that which is eternal (5:9 ff.; 8:31 ff.).

One of the crucial passages is Romans 3:21-26. One outstanding difficulty is the meaning of *ilasterion* ("propitiation") in verse 25 (KJV). Another problem is whether there is one consistent meaning of the "righteousness of God," or whether it has different meanings in passages such as verse 22 and verse 26. "Not that these two principal difficulties are unrelated to each other. On the contrary, they are inextricably intertwined, and cannot be discussed apart. It is an argument for distinguishing two senses of δικαιοσύνη θεοῦ (the righteousness of God) that when we do so we are enabled to see more clearly the meaning of ἱλαστήριος. It is the very function of Jesus Christ set forth by God as a propitiation in His blood to exhibit these two senses (which are equally indispensable if there is to be a religion for sinful men) in their unity and consistency with each other. And, on the other hand, the term ἱλαστήριος, to say the least, is relative to some problem created by sin for a God who would justify sinners; and the distinction of two senses in which δικαιοσύνη θεοῦ is used enables us to state this problem in a definite form."[93] There can be no gospel unless there is the presupposition of the righteousness of God extending to the ungodly. Then the question returns, How do you relate this righteous God to this sinful world? Paul sums up his solution to the problem by stating: "Christ Jesus: Whom God hath set forth to be a propitiation through faith in his blood . . ." (KJV). This is how God has acted to justify the ungodly who have accepted Jesus and yet retained his righteousness.

Denney maintains, and quite rightly so, that so many of the explanations of the death of Christ miss the point because they show no relation either to the freedom from the law or to existing controversies within his churches. This is precisely where so many Pauline theologians have been sidetracked.

The passage in Romans becomes simple as soon as we read it in the light of those we have already examined in 2 Corinthians and in Galatians. It is Christ set forth in His blood who is a propitiation; that is, it is Christ who died. In dying, as Paul conceived it, He made our sin His own. He took it on Himself as the reality which it is in God's sight and to God's law. He became sin, became a curse for us. It is this which gives His death a propitiatory character and power, which makes it possible, in other words, for God to be at once righteous and a God who accepts as righteous those who believe in Jesus. He is righteous, for in the death of Christ His law is honoured by the Son who takes the sin of the world to Himself as all that it is to God; and He can accept as righteous those who believe in Jesus, for in so believing sin becomes to them what it is to Him. I do not know any word which conveys the truth of this if "vicarious" or "substitutionary" does not. Nor do I know any interpretation of Christ's death which enables us to regard it as a demonstration of love to sinners, if this vicarious or substitutionary character is denied.[94]

The New Testament calls us to acknowledge this love as we look at the cross where Christ bore our sins and died our death. Hence, it is this love that constrains us. "Accepting this interpretation, we see that the *whole* secret of Christianity is contained in Christ's death, and in the believing abandonment of the soul to that death in faith. It is from Christ's death, and the love which it demonstrates, that all Christian inferences are drawn. . . . 'For if, while we were enemies, we were reconciled to God through the death of His Son, *much more,* being reconciled, shall we be saved by His life' (Rom. 5:8 ff.). . . . The propitiatory death of Christ, as an all-transcending demonstration of love, evokes in sinful souls a response which is *the whole of Christianity.* The love of Christ constraineth us: whoever can say that can say all that is to be said about the Christian life."[95]

There is really no argument that we can raise against the gospel that Paul gives, for it is not a philosophy. It was a matter of Paul's living out the context of his life and death under the dynamic relationship with a vital, caring God. The only objections that can be raised are from those individuals who have come as close to God as he has. It might be that if one ventured out as Paul did, his disagreements would depreciate as his respect increased. For as individuals, we still come to Paul seeing through a glass darkly. It is a witness to be borne out in a life of both servitude and gratitude. This life Paul best describes by means of baptism, in which individuals go down to sin in death but are transformed by the act and rise as new beings in fuller dimensions of life.

Paul sees death as a threefold concept: a death to sin, a death to flesh, and a death to law. Since Christ in fact died our death on the cross, the commitment to it also evokes a death. Christ's death first and foremost was a death for sin, because sin produced the situation that led to his death (6:10). "For us, dying to sin may seem to have a different meaning; it is not only a discharge from its responsibilities that is wanted, but a deliverance from its power. But this can come only on the foundation of the other; it is the discharge from the responsibilities of sin involved in Christ's death and appropriated in faith, which is the motive power in the daily ethical dying to sin. It really is such a motive power, and the only one in the world, when we realize what it is."[96]

Paul challenges us to take the whole matter of sin as seriously as Christ did in facing death. There must be an all-out drive of the individual to separate himself completely from sin. This would evoke within the individual a death unto sin through the whole of life. This calls for our daily mortification of evil.

We would thus in effect share in the crucifixion with Christ by daily taking up the cross against passion and lust.

Law has become impotent in regard to the flesh. It is a death to the flesh as stated in Romans 8:3-8. Flesh means "sin in its constitutional and instinctive character, sin as the nature or the second nature of man, it does not here matter which. What the law could not do God took another way of doing. He sent His Son in the likeness of flesh of sin, and as a sin-offering, and in so doing condemned sin in the flesh. ὁμοίωμα here no doubt emphasizes Christ's likeness to us: it is not meant to suggest difference or unreality in His nature."[97] Thus, by this manner of propitiation God did condemn sin in the flesh. His judgment was pronounced upon it in Christ's death, thereby ending both its nature and power. This death canceled the Law; it did to sin what the Law could never do, and that was to break its power.

Paul repeatedly refers to death for the Christian as a death to the law (Rom. 6:14; 7:4; Gal. 2:19). This is the point at which both critics and followers have done the most harm because they have misunderstood Paul.

On the one hand, when Christ died, justice was done to the law of God, both as an imperative and as a condemning law, as it had never been done before. The will of God had been honoured by a life of perfect obedience, and the awful experience of death in which God's inexorable judgment on sin comes home to the conscience had been borne in the same obedience and love by His sinless Son. On the other hand, when this death evokes the faith for which it appeals, the righteous requirement of the law is fulfilled in the believer; the law gets its due in his life also, or, as the apostle puts it, it is established by faith. How is it, then, that faith involves a death to the law? It is through the assurance, given to faith at the cross, that so far as doing the will of God is concerned a new and living way has been found.[98]

It is not the statutory law which was so cumbersome but rather the law transformed by the atonement. And it is the inspiration of Christ which directs the whole of Christian life, not the rigidity and confines of the law.

From this springs the liberty about which Paul talks. It is the same thing that Augustine meant when he asked us to love God and then do as we please. It is the perfect freedom to open oneself to the power and the glory of Christ's message. It is the freedom to fulfill the task for which we were called. It is the call to serve one whose service is perfect freedom. Thus, through the death of Christ and the atonement the individual is dead to the Law.

We are not just left as such. It is not simply a matter of working out our destiny with "fear and trembling," for we are given the Spirit. And it is the Spirit that relates us daily and directly to the, meaning of Christ's death for our own lives.

But if we are speaking of the new moral life of the Christian, and ask what we mean by the Spirit psychologically, that is, what form the experience of His work takes, I should say it is indistinguishable from that infinite assurance of God's love, given in Christ's death, through which the Christian is made more than conqueror in all the difficulties of life, inward or external. It is with this assurance that the Spirit is connected when Paul opens his discussion of the subject in Romans 5:5: "The love of God hath been shed abroad in our hearts through the Holy Spirit which was given unto us." With this same assurance he concludes his discussion in Romans 8:35: "Who shall separate us from the love of God?" The triumphant certainty of this love, a certainty always recurring to and resting on that miracle of miracles, the sin-bearing death of Christ, is the same thing as joy in the Holy Spirit, and it is this joy which is the Christian's strength. From the Spirit, then, or from the love of God as an assured possession, the Christian life may equally be explained. And it is not another, but the same explanation, when we say that it is begotten and sustained from beginning to end by the virtue which dwells in the propitiatory death of Jesus.[99]

The Letters of the Imprisonment

These letters constitute a new peak of Paul's writings. Before writing them he must have surveyed the whole of his work—the trials and tribulations, the persecutions and joys, as well as the failures and successes. The letter to the Philippians ties in readily with those to the Galatians and Romans; thus, even in the end he held tenaciously and consistently to his beliefs (Phil. 3:9-10). Within these letters Paul does not stray from the fundamental doctrines that he first maintained; it is rather a case of his bringing into focus the items on the fringes as his own faith defined the challenges confronting him.

He sees before him the whole world and all mankind in a much larger framework and larger scope as set against the universe as a whole. "God has been pleased 'through Him to reconcile all things unto Himself, having made peace through the blood of His cross; through Him, I say, whether things upon the earth, or things in the heavens' (Col. 1:20)."[100] Reconciliation is now seen in the context of history, for "you, who once were estranged and hostile in mind, doing evil deeds, he has now reconciled in his body of flesh by his death" (Col. 1:21-22; see also Eph. 1:7-10). Paul began his belief with the encounter with the Jesus (the historical Christ), but now the mysteries of Christ have been revealed to him as he conceives the end as "unit[ing] all things in him, things in [or above] heaven and things on earth" (Eph. 1:10). This larger scope of the world is countered by its part in the spiritual world, and the one has consequences that influence the other. Thus, sin has far-reaching factors which not only have interplay upon earth but also ramifications that extend to all nature. It is like a cancer that may start in any part of the system and will ultimately spread throughout.

The people to whom he wrote believed in "thrones and dominions and principalities and powers"; and although there may be a touch of indifference, not to say scorn, in some of his own allusions to the high-sounding names—for instance, in Eph. 1:21f.—they had some sort of reality for him too. There are passages like Col. 2:15, or those in which he refers to τὰ στοιχεῖα τοῦ κόσμου (Gal. 4:3; Col. 2:8), where he seems to connect the spiritual beings in question with the angels through whom the law was given (Gal. 3:19, Acts 7:53), and to represent the superseding of Judaism by Christianity as a victory of Jesus over these inferior but refractory powers to whom for a while the administration of human affairs, and especially of the immature, materialistic and legal stages of religion had been committed.[101]

However, if Paul had held strongly to these beliefs, they would probably have come up more frequently.

In these letters of imprisonment Paul raises Christ to cosmic significance. Christ has outgrown the concept of the second Adam and has become the head of the new humanity, as in the earlier letters (Rom. 5:12 ff.; 1 Cor. 15:45 ff.). "He is the centre of the universe. He is a person so great that Paul is obliged to reconstruct His whole world around him. He is the primary source of all creation, its principle of unity, its goal (Col. 1:15 ff.)."[102] His works permeate all the universe. He has come for all and has a claim on all.

What is of consequence is his conviction that in Jesus Christ dwelt all the fulness of the Godhead—all that makes God in the full sense of the term God—bodily, that is, in organic unity and completeness; and that the same completeness and finality belong to His reconciling work. "The blood of His cross": it is in this we find the resolution of all discords, not only in the life of man, but in the universe at large. It is in this we see a divine love which does not shrink from taking on itself to the uttermost the moral responsibility for the world it has made, for all the orders of being in it, and all their failures and fortunes.[103]

There will be a universal reconciliation when Jews and Gentiles have been made one through the body of Christ (Eph. 2:11-22). Here is one of the high points of Paul's thinking: God is not the God of the Jews only (Rom. 3:29). A God of such significance and supremacy cannot be working merely for one minority group. "On the contrary, there is nothing in the world so universally intelligible as the cross. Hence it is the meeting-place not only of God and man, but of all races and conditions of men with each other. There is neither Greek nor Jew, male nor female, bond nor free, there. The cross is the basis of a universal religion, and has in it the hope of a universal peace."[104]

In conclusion, one can say that the immediacy and hope of Jesus' early return have vanished. Paul no longer expects to be present to watch the Parousia but rather wants to press on "to depart and be with Christ" (Phil. 1:23). The kingdom of Christ will have an everlasting duration and all will be subject to his power. It is by faith in the righteousness of God through faith in Christ that Paul hopes to share in the power of Christ's resurrection and thus attain the resurrection from the dead (Phil. 3:10 ff.).

Not only is Christ raised to cosmic significance but he is the goal to which all creation is moving. All things are to be united in Christ (Eph. 1:10), and he will "reconcile to himself all things" (Col. 1:20). Thus, no trace of evil or wickedness will survive; it will be completely obliterated. It shall either bow before Christ's presence or be utterly destroyed.

Throughout these letters there is an entirely new growth and completeness not previously expressed. Paul is more settled in his own mind and has the opportunity to reflect clearly on the problems, an opportunity his earlier letters did not allow. His eschatology is bound up in a statement in Titus (3:4-7):[105] "when the goodness and loving kindness of God our Savior appeared, he saved us, not because of deeds done by us in righteousness, but in virtue of his own mercy, by the washing of regeneration and renewal in the Holy Spirit, which he poured out upon us richly through Jesus Christ our Savior, so that we might be justified by his grace and become heirs in hope of eternal life."

Summary

The eschatology of the New Testament is essentially the eschatology of Paul; hence, it is in the field of eschatology that Paul becomes the theologian *par excellence*. There are two reasons for this: first, he drowns out other competitors by sheer bulk; and second, he devotes the whole of his writing to eschatology. For Paul, eschatology was theology and theology was eschatology; the two were indivisible. There was no need to make these two fields into separate concepts; therefore, there was never any conscious attempt to develop their differences. It is to Paul that the church must turn time and time again to find the Christian meaning of both life and death, for in these matters Paul has become our authority and example.

Paul shared every moment of life with death. Death to him was not some vague metaphor but rather a personal experience since he was threatened by death so many times in his life. Again and again we see these fleeting references to threatening dangers and are never led directly to the details; yet from all of this we can certainly surmise that Paul's life was in constant danger. His conversion to Christianity represents one of the most radical changes that anyone could undergo. Because of this cleavage, he did not see himself so much as a continuous being but rather as one who had two radically distinct lives. He could speak of this in only the most severe and drastic terminology—as if he had "died." Paul's figurative language became a reality to him.

Paul started with the most offensive part of Christianity, namely, the crucifixion, and made it the very center of his gospel. And as he preached Christ and Christ crucified, the most repulsive account in the whole of Judaism, he found at the same time that it was also the most magnetic teaching he had yet encountered. The polarity of the cross had the power both to attract and to repel. It was the encounter with the risen Lord that became both the core and the content of his proclamation. Paul spoke of the "last things" first, not so much because of their imminence but because of their importance in his life and indeed in the life of those to follow. For out of the resurrection of Christ there came an entirely new situation. By his death he rang in a new age. As all the descendants of Adam shared in the certain death of inheritance, so through Christ all shall be made alive.

The resurrection of Christ ushers in a new age of a new world. As one being first born from the dead, he gives rise to a new expectation and an intensely deepened relationship with the Father. All of this is new because it is centered on the resurrection of Christ as the final guarantor. If the resurrection is true, for those who dare to think consistently, we are now in the supernatural age. This is Paul's point of view, and all Christian thinking must be thought out in terms of it. The church can no longer exist when it stops believing in the resurrection, the ground and core of its existence. Without this belief it has a purely illegitimate existence. Christianity without resurrection, for Paul, is a lie and a deceit, not because it is without this article of faith, but because it is in itself an illusion, a fiction. If one attempts to escape from the resurrection as the alleged absurd, he is sawing off the branch upon which he is sitting.

The concepts of Gehenna and its torments are conspicuous by their absence. We know that Paul was nurtured in rabbinic thought, which continually upheld the symbols of eternal fire. Yet, here he is silent. Nothing could be more profound than this. In doing this he sets himself over against Judaism, the Synoptic tradition, and the teachings of Jesus. It must be at once apparent that Paul could not endorse or promote the concept of perpetual torment, which Jesus may have supported.

Paul believed that the most tragic event that could confront an individual was that he might die after he was dead. This means that as an individual he would be given over to irrevocable death rather than the converse of eternal life. This indeed was much more to be feared than anything that we might imagine. Paul believed that unregenerate men were already "dead" in this world and as such were under the bondage of "decay" and "perdition," but there was always the strong hope that they might arouse themselves to an awareness and change their state before it became too late. Until the last he spoke of those who were lost, whose end was perdition, but he became less and less able to set limits on the reconciling energy of God in Jesus Christ the Lord.

It was the divine encounter with Christ which forced Paul to reconsider the Jesus of history. He stood at the end of Christ's life and had to reshape it from entirely new criteria, all of which became transformed and developed into depth of spirit and thought for Paul. It was Paul's thought that transformed the ugly wooden cross of an idealist's death into the supreme altar of the Christian faith. There were never on the lips of Paul any kind words for death since it stood diametrically opposed to God and his plans. Death was the ultimate in evil, yet before the power of God even death had to quiver. Death is the fearful separation from God. It then pronounces the last word on man's fate and destiny, and hence it always speaks of doom. To Paul's mind there could be no more grievous penalty for sin than death, the death that would mean banishment from God and complete paralysis of the individual.

It was sin that caused God to enter this world in the person of Christ, and it was sin that made Christ's death a necessity in order to reveal God's love as well as Christ's. It was only by sin that death held any power over us and it was only by Jesus' wrestling with evil that he could effectually accept our responsibility—and die for us.

Christ's death was a complete act of obedience to the will of the Father. It was not obedience merely in the sense of doing the will of God as other men were called to do it, the everyday keeping of God's commandments; it was obedience in this unique and incommunicable, yet moral, calling to be, at the cost of life, the Savior of the world. Therefore, it was in the obedience of Christ to the Father that the great demonstration of his love to men was given. "[He] loved me," the apostle says, "and gave himself for me." It is with this same mind that Paul could move forward and confront both life and death by saying, "Wherefore, O King Agrippa, I was not disobedient to the heavenly vision" (Acts 26:19).

Salvation has entered the world and is working toward the end that Christ will come again, there will be the resurrection of the dead, followed by the last judgment, and concluded when God becomes "all in all." This is the constant vision that Paul finds behind his whole concept of life and what he believes will happen after death. From these basic concepts he did not change one iota. While he continued to mature in faith and insight, the very center of his kerygma continued as a constant. Even the strong elements of Hellenistic ideas never swayed or colored his views concerning the doctrines of the last things. In the last analysis, the essence of the basic dogmas was not in flux, but Paul attempted to bring into sharper focus some of the fuzzier details.

Increasingly Paul's entire doctrine concerning the "last things" became dominated by the theme of "being with the Lord." Death for Jesus or even for Paul was neither attractive nor necessarily a positive gain. The early church bore witness to this and Paul would also. But beyond the experience of death he would be at one "with Christ" in a newer, deeper, more intimate way than he had ever known possible. This certainly held more for him than any aspect of this life. And so it was to be "with the Lord" that Paul could look past this life to the life to come in power and in fullness when he shall never be separated from the Lord. As Paul moved closer and closer to his Lord, the bond of Christ's love grew strong and certain, breaking all bonds not of love.

3

The Concept of Death
in the
Johannine Writings

*. . . the Christian heart is sensible of all it owes
to Him, and sensible that it owes it all in some
way to His death.*

—James Denney

ONE OF the unifying factors of the corpus of Johannine writings is the strong bent toward eschatology. John does not run from the eschatology of the New Testament, rather,

he has emphasized its truth, and at the same time emphasized its problems and inadequacies, perhaps more strongly than any other writer. Eschatology is least inadequate in figurative description of the final end and goal of history. It gives a tolerable account of the work and person of Jesus, which in any case are paradoxical. It is least satisfactory in dealing with the age of the Church, the interval which lies between the adumbration of the end in Jesus and the end itself. This age however is the age which John was primarily concerned to explain, and it was the necessity

For the purpose of simplicity the writings in the New Testament attributed to John will be dealt with in this chapter. Recent scholarship in this area would seem to indicate that this is perhaps more practical and realistic than what was believed at the turn of the century. However, it is the theology not the authorship that this chapter wishes to examine. In the pattern of Archdeacon R. H. Charles and Professor James Denney, the Apocalypse will be examined first, followed by an evaluation of the Gospel and the letters.

of explaining it which, more than any other factor, led to the development of his theology. Johannine theology is not so much the imposition of alien forms and terminology upon primitive Christian thought (though it is expressed partly in new forms and terminology), as the spontaneous development of primitive Christian thought under the pressure of inner necessity and the lapse of time.[1]

It is readily seen that the terminology of this corpus is *loaded*. The term *loaded* here means that the words are used as vehicles to convey meanings far beyond the normal meanings. These nuances become the means by which the theology of John is expressed. No biblical author or authors were as adept at using words as symbols, parables, or signs as was John. No New Testament writer was quite so quick to relate the whole of Christian thought to the Greek world. This is not so surprising when we reflect that it was John who had a deep and abiding respect for the Word and the words of God.

The Word of God for John was a dynamic, creative, life-giving, light-giving force which seeks out men in order that they might find a right relationship with God, and which seeks to hold them there.[2] By his Word was the world created and brought into being. Thus, it was John's high and holy thought that this same Jesus was not a word from God in the sense of an ongoing revelation, but rather Jesus was the very Word of God. This infers that Jesus was not only God's first word to man but also his last word. Jesus as the Word is God's fullest and finest revelation. Because of this great interest in semantics and revelation, we are assured that John's words are clear, cogent, and consistent, making it possible for us to learn what he intended.

Whatever words John might have used to accomplish his task, the theme remains a constant; it is simply the love of God. Nowhere do we find a more succinct expression of this than in John 3:16. Death can no longer remain an abstraction, for the love of God has made man's relation to death the most subjective element in the universe.

Everything, we have seen, comes from the love of God. The death of Christ is to be construed in harmony with this, not in any antagonism to it. But the love of God to the world is never conceived in Scripture abstractly. . . . The giving of the Son includes at least the giving of Him to that death which, as we have seen, pervades the Gospel from beginning to end; indeed, the death is emphasized in the immediate context (3:14ff.). Nor are we left without sufficiently clear hints as to the necessity which determined the gift. In the passage just referred to (3:16) we see that apart from it men are lost; they perish, instead of having eternal life. John's mind revolves round these ultimate ideas, death and life, rather than their moral equivalents or presuppositions, sin and righteousness. But we cannot suppose that he did not include in "death" and "life" all that we mean by these latter words.[3]

These "ultimates" communicate depths of insight that are still obscure to our minds. Here, then, John expresses the inscrutable mysteries of God in terms that are applicable and lasting. It was John's task not to project Christians into the future but rather to make the future active and present in the daily activities of the church.

The Apocalypse

Moving on from these general considerations of the Johannine corpus, we shall consider the Apocalypse in detail. Here one finds himself immersed by a "new heaven" and a "new earth" in linguistic symbols. As a background for his writings, John used 1 Enoch, the Twelve Testaments, the Gospels of Mark and Matthew, and something of Paul. Even though he used 1 Enoch considerably and the Old Testament greatly, his work is not dependent upon them. A wide and diverse stream of literature and wisdom flows through the Apocalypse; it stands as a unity in and of itself. Dr. Austin Farrer states that John never attempted to copy sources, but fully digested his material and came out with a real grasp of the ancient scriptures.[4]

The Apocalypse stands as a monument to apocalyptic literature. The same symbols are used, yet John stands in view of the accomplished mission, the end. The message of John is a high point of Christian theology because he moves far beyond the thoughts of the Old Testament writers. John has seen the end of history and writes from that vantage point; to him has been revealed the true meaning of history. Even though he has been proved to be not completely accurate about history, his insights into the fundamentals of the Christian faith give an eternal significance, which is operative in every age, making the message always contemporaneous with history.

The writing is never impaired by the narrow scope of the needs for which it was written. There is absolutely no doubt in John's mind that the church will win out in Victory. In spite of all the troubles and fears, God has the last word. John's complete trust in God as Author and Finisher, as Creator and Redeemer in this life and the next, is unsurpassed in the Scriptures. So too is the nature of his language, which makes the Apocalypse absolutely unique.

This symbolism was the only means open to express the conflicts between Christ and Caesar, between the church and the world, and between God and the demonic. John here is not really concerned with the symbolism itself or from where it came. His concern is only to set forth the glory of God in the slain lamb as it was revealed to him. The symbolism of the symbols became more real than reality to John. The warp and woof of the symbolism is ancient, but from these threads and his unsurpassed skill he weaves a new pattern which is *sui generis*. It stands at the end of a great continuum of apocalyptic literature, but it is far greater because it fully and finally ends this literature with the appearance of Jesus Christ. It is no mere revelation; it is *The Revelation*. Martin Kiddle states: "No matter what further information may be gleaned concerning John in the future, it cannot add to or take away from the value of the message as he has delivered it."[5] The value of the book

lies in the splendid energy of its faith, in the unfaltering certainty that God's own cause is at issue now and here and must ultimately prevail, and that the cause of Jesus Christ is inseparably linked therewith, and the main aim of which, as is clear from every page, is to emphasise the overwhelming worth of things spiritual as contrasted with things material—a lesson never more needed than at present—and in the next place to glorify martyrdom, to encourage the faithful to face death with constancy, nay more with rapturous joy: "Blessed are the dead that die in the Lord."[6]

Thus, in the face of death and persecution the book of Revelation comes as a means of encouragement. The members of the church have the Victory. John, who has seen the ultimate end, testifies and proclaims that even though death may hold its sway, it is God who has won the battle.

In the vision John had of Jesus, the latter was not immediately perceived by John. If we follow the spirit of these writings, we are aware that this was not the same Jesus of Nazareth, whom John perhaps knew. Now there was a tremendous difference, for what John saw was Jesus the Christ, the risen and ascended Lord, exalted in glory and in power. Christ moved forward to calm John, for the Lord of glory was the same Jesus of Nazareth—there was no need to fear. Here stood the Eternal One, the Ancient of Days, the firstborn from the dead, and the Alpha and Omega. The glory of the Lord shone around him and he was afraid because he had seen the Divine. One who had broken through the bonds of death came back to show the Way.

The whole activity at this point is the tremendous demonstration of love. "But he (John) cannot contemplate Him, nor think of the grace and peace which he invokes on the churches from Him, without recurring to the great deed of Christ on which they ultimately depend. . . . He does not say, 'who liberates us from our sins', as though a progressive purification were in view; but 'who liberated us', pointing to a finished work."[7] It was love that paid the price in terms of blood shed. Thus, one finds that "Christianity is as real as the blood of Christ. It is as real as the agony in the garden and the death on the cross. It is not less real than this, nor more real; it has no reality whatever which is separable from these historical things."[8]

The activity of Christ in his redeeming love can be known only through the subjective encounter, which must always remain self-authenticating. Through the process of redemption John maintained we are bound together as ones who acknowledge the rule of God over us. " 'He made us priests' means that in virtue of His action we are constituted a worshipping people of God; on the ground of it we have access to the Father. . . . All dignity and all privilege rest on the fact that He set us free from our sins at the cost of His blood. . . . The vision of Christ calls out the whole contents of the Christian consciousness; the Christian heart is sensible of all it owes to Him, and sensible that it owes it all in some way to His death."[9] To pry farther than this is unaskable; this is precisely where faith meets the believer.

The emphasis for Jesus is on fulfilling the role of the Lamb of God. This title appears some twenty-nine times. Here is an attempt to see Jesus almost exclusively in terms of Hebrew sacrifice. "It has the character which sacrifice confers, but it is alive. Although it is not dead, it has the virtue of its death in it. It is on the ground of this death, and of the redemption (or purchase of men for God) effected by it, that all praise is ascribed to the Lamb, and the knowledge and control of all providence put into His hands."[10] This, then, is the Ultimate display of love.

The nature of John's theology is conveyed in the theme of the Lamb of God, seen as One who takes away the sin of the world. "When sin is taken away by a lamb, it is taken away sacrificially. It is borne off by being in some sense (in the case of an unintelligent sacrifice, only a figurative sense) borne. It is not too much to say that the conception of Christ's death as a sacrifice for sin, found thus, at the very beginning of the Gospel, on the lips of the great witness to Jesus, is meant to convey decisively the evangelist's own conception of Jesus and His work. He is here to put away sin. That sums up His vocation. And He puts it away by a sacrifice in which it has to be borne."[11]

The theology of the Lamb of God being sacrificed brings out three important concepts. The first is the concept of the Lamb who was obedient unto death. This theme is parallel to the concept of obedience lifted up by Paul's writings. "This spontaneity on the part of Jesus, when it is put in relation to the love of the Father in giving the Son, appears as obedience. The authority or liberty He has to lay down His life and to take it again is a commandment He has received from the Father. Equally with Paul or with the writer to the Hebrews, John could use the term 'obedience' to describe the whole work of Christ. But as with them, so with him too, it is loving obedience to a will of love, an attitude at once to God's purpose and to man's need which makes the passion the sublimest of actions, and justifies the paradox of the gospel that the cross is a 'lifting up' or a glorifying of Jesus."[12] The obedience of the Lamb to the very end makes the sacrifice efficacious.

The second concept concerns the morality of the sacrifice. Previously the Jews had used an unblemished lamb which was bound and offered as a sacrifice. Conversely, the Lamb of God had free will. At any point Jesus could have turned from the task and would have been released gladly. "The perfect freedom with which Christ acts the shepherd's part, including the final sacrifice which it demands, is apparently the characteristic of His work to which he attaches the greatest importance. And it is so because it is through the freeness with which the surrender of life is made that the love which is its motive is revealed. 'I lay down My life of Myself. No one taketh it from Me. I have authority to lay it down, and I have authority to take it again.' "[13] Jesus died the sacrificial death because it became his will to do so. This lifts the death of Jesus to a high level of morality, which was not a part of the traditional theology of the Jewish sacrifice.

The third point is that the whole aspect of the Lamb of God can be seen correctly only from the perspective of the love of God.

But the love of God to the world is never conceived in Scripture abstractly. It is not manifested in some evolutionary process which is necessarily determined *a priori,* as some may have hastily inferred from the prologue to this Gospel. To conceive it so would be to deny its grace. It is conceived, practically, in relation to definite needs of man which it meets. It is manifested not on the analogy of natural forces, which simply are what they are, but on the analogy of the free actions of men, which are determined by specific motives. To deny this is to lose the living and gracious

God of revelation, and to take in His place a metaphysical phantom. God so loved the world that He gave His only begotten Son.[14]

This is the love of God expressed in his omnipotence. The slain Lamb appears to be the most powerful instrument in the universe. Here, then, is the paradox: the Lamb, having been slain, weak from the loss of blood, destroyed the combination of forces for mankind. Thus, the weakness of God is stronger than the strength of men. The Lamb of God in its traditional symbolism conveys magnificently the whole work of Christ.

The death of the Lamb of God in its empirical form is a martyr's death. This is the example for all followers who would be obedient unto death. "The typical Christian is a martyr too. To be a martyr is to furnish the decisive proof that the abiding power of Christ's blood is being exercised over one's life. . . . Hence the blood of Christ does something both once for all, in breaking the bond by which sin holds us and bringing us into such a relation to God that we are a people of priests, and progressively, in assuring our gradual assimilation to Jesus Christ the faithful witness. In both respects the Christian life is absolutely indebted to it; without it, it could neither begin nor go on."[15]

Out of the trials and tribulations will come many martyrs. The blood of the Lamb will cleanse them and they will be sanctified. Just how this formula works we are not told.

The pressure put on them [the martyrs] would have been too great, and they would inevitably have succumbed to it. But with a motive behind them like the blood of the Lamb they were invincible. Now nothing can be a motive unless it has a meaning; nothing can be a motive in the sense implied here unless it has a gracious meaning. . . . With the cross on which He died for them before their eyes, they dared not betray His cause by cowardice, and love their own lives more than He had loved His. They must be His, as He had been theirs. It is taken for granted here that in the blood of the Lamb there had been a great demonstration of love to them. . . . It is because it is an incomparable demonstration of love that it is an irresistible motive. And though the relation is not thought out nor defined here, for such a definition would have been utterly out of place, it is not forcing the language in the least to assume that it must have existed in fact for the author.[16]

The revelation that John receives is a forewarning of the Parousia. Christ addresses himself to the various churches of that day as well as those of today. Christ's presence shows that he stands over against them in judgment because he knows their works and that his last coming to rectify the world is imminent. The church is left in watchful expectation, and it is filled with an air of repentance. "Remember then what you received and heard; keep that, and repent" (3:3). " 'Behold, I am coming soon, bringing my recompense, to repay every one for what he has done. . . .Surely I am coming soon.' Amen. Come, Lord Jesus!" (22:12, 20). These writings are filled with the eager and honest expectation of his coming. He will come in power, symbolized by the clouds, which will usher forth a great day. "The judgment of the great day—'the great day of God' (16:14)—is represented under the image of illimitable slaughter, before the beginning of which the birds of prey are summoned to feast on the bodies and blood of men (19:17, 18, 21; cf. 14:20)."[17]

At the final judgment the Antichrists will be thrown into the lake of fire and their adherents will be slain. "The 'lake of fire' in which this 'second death' is experienced, and into which the devil, the beast, and the false prophet are cast, has its torments 'day and night for ever and ever.' It is exclusion from 'the marriage supper of the Lamb,' from 'the holy city,' from the fellowship of God in His 'tabernacle with men.' It is the death that is beyond all other death. It means existence without the resurrection of life and the crown of life, the existence that is eternal loss and dying."[18]

Satan, having lost all his cohorts on earth, stands powerless. He is then bound with chains for a thousand years (20:1-3).

Thereupon ensues the Millennium, when the martyrs, and the martyrs only, are raised in the first resurrection and become priests of God (cf. Is. 61:6) and of Christ, and reign with Christ personally on earth for a thousand years (20:4-6), with Jerusalem as the centre of the kingdom. According to an earlier passage (5:10) they are made unto God "a kingdom and priests; and they reign upon the earth."[19]

So that individuals might "share in the blessings of the millennial reign of Christ the souls of the martyrs are raised up; they live and reign with Christ a thousand years (20:4, 6). This is called 'the first resurrection'. Those raised up are untouched by the second death; they are the priests of God and of Christ (20:5, 6) and reign upon the earth (5:10). The rest of the dead do not live again until the thousand years are finished (20:5)."[20]

It is worth noting that this is the only passage in the entire New Testament where the doctrine of the millennium is explicitly written. Certainly this one isolated passage cannot be used to sustain an important Christian doctrine. The doctrine itself "in its present form, I repeat, that is, in its combination of the resurrection of the martyrs with a temporary Messianic kingdom under the Christian Messiah. In our earlier chapters we saw that when once the Messianic kingdom came to be regarded as temporary, from that moment—more than 150 years before the date of the New Testament Apocalypse—the resurrection was relegated from the beginning of the Messianic kingdom to its close, and the righteous were conceived as rising not to the Messianic kingdom, but to eternal blessedness in a new world or in heaven itself."[21]

Edward Langton takes this same point of view when he states: "From the account of the New Testament teaching that has been given above, it is evident that the doctrine of the Millennium is not an essential feature of Christianity. It does not find any place in the most authoritative sources of Christian teaching. Not only is it true that no reference is made to it outside the Apocalypse. What is more impressive is the fact that no place is allowed by the writers for such an interval in their eschatological scheme of events, for the Second Advent and the last judgment follow immediately upon each other."[22]

At the end of this thousand-year reign of the messianic kingdom, Satan will be freed. Then "the nations Gog and

Magog—the idea goes back ultimately to Ezek. 38:2—39:16—are stirred up to make the last assault on the kingdom of Christ (Rev. 20:7-9): 'And when the thousand years are finished, Satan shall be loosed out of his prison, and shall come forth to deceive the nations which are in the four corners of the earth, Gog and Magog, to gather them together to war: the number of whom is as the sand of the sea. And they went up over the breadth of the earth, and compassed the camp of the saints about, and the beloved city.' In this attack they are destroyed by God Himself, who sends down fire from heaven (20:9). The devil is finally cast into the lake of fire (20:10), where are also the Beast and the false prophet."[23]

At the end of this millennium, God takes his place on his great white throne to judge the world. "God is Judge, and yet in some respects the Messiah also (22:12): 'Behold I come quickly; and my reward is with me, to render to each man according as his work is' (cf. also 6:16, 17). All are judged according to their works, which stand revealed in the heavenly books (20:12). The wicked are cast into the lake of fire (21:8; see also 19:20, 20:10). So likewise are death and Hades (20:14). Hades seems to be conceived in the Apocalypse as the intermediate abode of the wicked only; for it is always combined with death (see 1:18, 6:8, 20:13, 14)."[24]

The souls of the martyrs are aggregated in a place beneath the altar. John takes a rather negative outlook on the vocation of the martyrs because they spend their time praying for the destruction of those who persecuted them. The other faithful people are assigned to paradise. Then they are aggregated in a place beneath the altar. There is to be the second death, which is the "death of the soul, as the first is the death of the body. It is not the annihilation, but the endless torment of the wicked that is here meant. The expression is a familiar Rabbinic one (see Jerusalem Targ. on Deut. 33:6, where for 'let Reuben live and not die,' we have 'let Reuben live and not die the second death')."[25]

The end will come finally as a new world is brought about by the combination of a new heaven and a new earth plus the heavenly Jerusalem. "Then the ideal kingdom of God becomes actual. This city needs no temple; for God and Christ dwell in it (21:22). The throne of God and of the Lamb is set up therein (22:1, 3). The citizens dwell in perfect fellowship with God (22:4), and are as kings unto God (22:5). The Messiah still exercises His mediatorial functions (see 7:17, 21:22, 23, etc.)."[26]

There is to be a distinction between Jews and Gentiles, which will be of a spiritual nature. "The redeemed of Israel are to dwell in the New Jerusalem, while the Gentiles are to walk in the light thereof (21:24, 26). The former are to eat of the fruit of the tree of life, while the latter are to be healed by its leaves (22:2). The twelve gates of the heavenly city are to be named after the twelve tribes (21:12), and the names of the twelve Apostles are inscribed on the foundation stone of the city. Yet Jew and Gentile form one divine community, and are alike kings and priests unto God (1:6, 5:10)."[27]

The Gospel According to John

The Gospel According to John was written to tell of the life, death, resurrection, and lordship of Jesus Christ. The author seems to look and write for those who see with the "eye of faith" so that they might grow in faith. These accounts "are written that you may believe that Jesus is the Christ, the Son of God, and that believing you may have life in his name" (20:31). The theme is an invitation—"Come and see, come and see"— rising to a *crescendo* until it turns to a challenge—"Follow me, follow me." A person is thus introduced to the reader—not just another person but rather one who is presented as being uniquely the Son of God. He is of such magnitude that he stands before all creation. An offer of Eternal Life is made to those who wish to participate in the inscrutable riches of God. The response that is required is acceptance of Jesus as the Way, the Truth, and the Life. John thus relegates to Jesus the position of being One with the Father. It was John's gracious thought that Jesus stands as the Word made flesh.

The presence of eternal life seems to arise first from who Jesus was rather than what he did, as seen in the prologue. "Jesus redeems men, or gives them life, by revealing to them

147

the truth about God. The revelation is made in His own person, by His words and deeds, no doubt, but supremely by what He is. 'This is life eternal, that they should know Thee the only true God, and Him whom Thou didst send, even Jesus Christ' (17:3). The work of redemption, to borrow the dogmatic category, is interpreted through the prophetic office of Christ almost exclusively."[28]

W. F. Howard interprets eternal life in this way: " 'The actual impartation of the actual life of God is the core of the Johannine soteriology. It is this that makes the Gospel a gospel, and Christ the mediator of a real salvation. "This is the witness, that God gave us eternal life, and this life is in his Son." ' Thus Robert Law sums up the meaning of salvation as it is set before us in the writings of St. John. It is evident that, just as St. Paul found the central message of Christianity in salvation, which he illustrated by figures taken from the law courts, or from the temple where slaves paid the ransom price for their manumission, so for St. John eternal life is the supreme gift of God brought to man by Christ Jesus."[29]

The concept of Life and eternal life is best demonstrated in the account of the raising of Lazarus. This will be examined in greater detail later, but it must now be seen as an expression of the meaning of eternal life.

The doctrine of eternal life is stated in two forms. First: "He who believes in me, even if he dies, will come to life" (giving to *zesetai* the ingressive sense which properly belongs to the form). This may be taken as a confirmation of the popular eschatology as enunciated by Martha: faith in Christ gives the assurance that the believer will rise again after death. But the second statement is not the simple equivalent of this: "Everyone who is alive and has faith in me will never die." The implication is that the believer is already "living" in a pregnant sense which excludes the possibility of ceasing to live. In other words, the "resurrection" of which Jesus has spoken is something which may take place before bodily death, and has for its result the possession of eternal life here and now.[30]

The believer who " 'hears my word and believes on Him who sent me possesses eternal life, and he does not come to judgment, but *has passed* from death into life. I solemnly assure you, the time is coming, *and now is,* when the dead will hear the voice of the Son of Man, and they who hear will come to life.' It is because the word of Christ has this power here and now that we can believe that it will have the same power hereafter. . . . The evangelist agrees with popular Christianity that the believer will enter into eternal life at the general resurrection, but for him this is a truth of less importance than the fact that the believer already enjoys eternal life, and the former is a consequence of the latter."[31] This, then, is the controlling and sustaining factor of the Christian faith, that is, the individual can participate in that which is from beyond.

Basically "the 'eternal' is a qualitative term, not a quantitative; used not in order to add to the 'life' the idea of *perpetuity,* but to express more fully the quality which belongs to the 'life' itself. In John's writings 'death' is an ethical condition, the condition of failure and evil in which men exist by nature, and out of which they are raised by Christ."[32]

Thus, the values of Christianity are a present-day occurrence. This is what makes all the difference for John: whether one stands in a relationship to Life and Light or to death and darkness. The various passages that John uses to speak of eternal life "affirm, first, that eternal life may be enjoyed here and now by those who respond to the word of Christ, and, secondly, that the same power which assures eternal life to believers during their earthly existence will, after the death of the body, raise the dead to renewed existence in a world beyond."[33]

The concept of Life (Ζωή or Zoē) is presented in the fullest and most radical way in the writings of John. He relates all of Christian theology to this basic concept of Life. Thus, this becomes an all-inclusive term related to the very act of creation. Jesus not only possesses Life but is the source of all Life and also the source and validity behind all faith.

However, since, as the revealer, he is and gives ζωή (I John 1:1f.), and since it was with his coming that ζωή was revealed, believers already have ζωή as a present fact in faith. The paradoxical nature of this assertion is expressly stressed: whoever believes has already passed from death into life (5:24; I John 3:14); now, as he is speaking (and for the evangelist that also means every occasion when the Word is proclaimed) the eschatological hour takes place (5:25). He is, as the speaker, the ἀνάστασις and the ζωή, so that whoever believes in him lives, though he might die; indeed, in the true sense, he will not die at all (11:25). He has already given the δόξα to his own in the revelation (17:22). Correspondingly, the promises relating to the future do not refer to a later eschatological future, but to the moment of decision when confronted with the Word. Whoever believes shall live. Yet, at the same time, this ζωή is not understood in the timeless, idealist sense. It is ζωή that has an everlasting future (4:14, 6:27, 12:25), and his own people, to whom he has given his δόξα, are nevertheless directed to the future vision of δόξα in fellowship with the glorified Son (17:24).[34]

The enigmatic statement about individuals who die but do not die at all can be seen only from the ultimate concept. This implies that when they die, their deaths are apparently the same as deaths of those outside the faith. Over against this natural death, God will ultimately restore them. Of course, this can be understood only after one has dismissed the limitations imposed by time.

It is certainly not important that the individual Christian comprehend all the implications of the concept of ζωή (Life). One can assume that even John did not begin to comprehend all that might be implied by his words. The motivation of his writings is to get the individual to have a subjective experience that will transform life to Life.

The essential thing, at any rate, is to understand the present nature of ζωή. Just as it is not an ideal entity, so also it does not consist of an inward spiritual life, as, for example, in a mystic sense. For John did not spiritualize the primitive Christian eschatology and thereby dissolve it, but, rather, in the same tradition as Jesus and Paul, radicalised it. That is, he took seriously the idea that the coming of Jesus as the revealer is the decisive eschatological event, the κρίσις. It is not in relation to an idea or a suprahistorical, metaphysical being, but by adhering in faith to an historical fact and an historical person that ζωή is attained, and, correspondingly, this life consists in the manner of an historical existence, in the certainty that comes through the word of revelation, which teaches one to understand any given moment in a new way, free from the past and open to the future. Life is at the same time the way and the objective.[35]

Some scholars have maintained that the Gospel of John contains less Jewish eschatology than do the other New Testament books. However, this Gospel was written with a very strong and thoughtful eschatological point of view. If one believes that eschatology means the ongoing catastrophes and the final consummation in a catastrophic ending, it must be said that this is not what John had in mind. The import of this writing is to bring these activities into the "here and now." Thus, the crisis or catastrophe becomes personal and subjective.

Jesus as the Son of Man is commissioned with the functions of Judge and Giver of life. The spatial background of thought is the old Jewish apocalyptic contrast between the world above and the world below. The temporal framework of thought is partly concealed, but there are traces of the distinction between the two ages, the present age and the age to come. For it should not be overlooked that in such a passage as John 12:25 ("he that loveth his life loseth it; and he that hateth his life in this world shall keep it unto life eternal"), that favourite term in the Johannine vocabulary, "eternal life," is eschatological in its origin. In rabbinic language two technical terms are used antithetically, hā 'ōlām hazzeh and hā 'ōlām habbā. These are equivalent to ὁ αἰών ὁ ἐνεστώς or ὁ κόσμος οὗτος, and to ὁ αἰων ὁ μελλων. Now the term "eternal life," ζωή αἰώνιος, has the meaning, "life in the coming age," and it is understood so in the passage just quoted. In the same connection we should notice that chronological indications of τὸ ἔσχατον run through the Gospel. "The hour is not yet"; "the hour is coming and now is." Nor must we overlook the significance of the sublime cry from the cross, τετέλεσται. Nothing, however, is more remarkable than the recurring refrain in the sixth chapter: "And I will raise him up at the last day."[36]

The Gospel contains only three references to the kingdom of God. It is simple for John to use this term, for it is either implicit or synonymous with "eternal life." "So in the Synoptics 'to inherit eternal life' and 'to enter into the Kingdom of God' seem to be interchangeable terms. But whereas the Kingdom is the favourite expression in the Synoptics, Eternal Life, or simply Life, is the constantly recurring phrase in John. It is indeed true that the characteristic use of this term by St. John removes it from the region in which it took its rise. But the passage just quoted (John 3:36) sets it in sharp antithesis to the wrath of God, ἡ ὀργή, which (as the Pauline epistles witness) was a technical term in Jewish eschatology."[37]

R. H. Charles states that although the concept of the kingdom is only mentioned as such, it is certainly present in all the teachings. "The divine gift of eternal life, as the good of the individual, can only be realised in so far as it brings the individual into vital union with the divine community, which is none other than the kingdom. The realisation of this life leads to unity with the brethren, such as prevails between the Father and the Son (17:21), and, through this unity consciously apprehended, the individual life attains to its perfection (17:23). Thus eternal life and the kingdom are correlative and complementary thoughts in the fourth Gospel. The indispensable evidence of this life in the individual is his love to the community. He who possesses it not has no divine life as an individual; he neither comes from God nor knows Him (I John 3:10, 4:8), but abides in darkness and death (I John 2:10, 3:14)."[38]

What, then, does death mean to John? "In John's writings 'death' is an ethical condition, the condition of failure and evil in which men exist by nature, and out of which they are raised by Christ. The 'life' is the new condition—the spiritual order of being, the existence of fellowship with God into which Christ brings men; and the 'eternal life' is this 'life' in its quality of the divine order of life, the life which fulfils the whole idea of life, the good of life, the perfection of life, the satisfaction of life in God."[39] Death is not just a natural event to be found at the culmination of living for Jesus. "Christ's death is not an incident of His life, it is the aim of it. The laying down of His life is not an accident in His career, but His vocation; in it the divine purpose of His life is revealed."[40] It was in, through, and by death that Jesus was able to redeem mankind.

The account of the resurrection of Lazarus adds a new

depth to the concept of Life which Christ gives. There is here a radical change in the nature of things: "that the gift of life is here presented expressly as victory over death. Resurrection is the reversal of the order of mortality, in which life always hastens towards death. The Hellenistic society to which this gospel was addressed was haunted by the spectacle of φθορά, the process by which all things pass into nothingness, and which engulfs all human existence. . . . Christ overcame death in dying. If therefore the episode of the Raising of Lazarus is to be a true σημεῖον of resurrection, it must in some way find place for the dying of Christ by virtue of which He is revealed as the resurrection and the life."[41]

The Lazarus account must be seen in light of being a precursor of Christ's death. "Thus the narrative before us is not only the story of dead Lazarus raised to life; it is also the story of Jesus going to face death in order to conquer death. In the previous episode we were told that the Good Shepherd comes to give life to His flock, and that in doing so He lays down His life for the sheep (10:10-11). The episode we are now considering conforms exactly to that pattern."[42] The death of Jesus was the death of an activist. ". . . it became clear that while on the one side His death is a free act of self-sacrifice, on the other side it is the assault of the powers of darkness upon the Light."[43]

The Good Shepherd account, coupled with the concept of the seed, which must be dissolved, points to the necessity of Christ's death. " 'I am the Good Shepherd: the Good Shepherd layeth down His life for the sheep' (10:11). This, it might be said, is only an ideal way of putting it; it is what the Good Shepherd would do if the situation emerged which required it. But it is not so recorded by the evangelist. The need has emerged, and the laying down of His life with a view to its resumption is made the sum and substance of the vocation of Jesus. 'Therefore doth the Father love Me, because I lay down My life, that I may take it again. No one taketh it away from Me, but I lay it down of Myself. I have power to lay it down, and I have power to take it again. This commandment received I from My Father' (10:17f.)."[44] The Good Shepherd is "good" precisely because he is willing to give up his life not only for his own sheep but also for the "other sheep" so that there might be one flock.

The account of the seed states that the seed must disintegrate so that there might be a crop. "Without the 'death' of the seed, no crop: without the death of Christ, no world-wide gathering of mankind. This strikes the key-note of the whole discourse."[45] Though the seed is a distinct entity and separate from the crops that it will produce, yet there is a relationship with, and a determination of, the crops which will be developed. The necessity to provide for the whole "crop" is contingent directly on the very death of Jesus. His death must be provided for the many.

In close connection with this there is the anticipation of the near and awful future, the shadow of which struck dark and cold upon the Saviour's soul. "Now is My soul troubled; and what shall I say? Father, save Me from this hour. But for this cause came I unto this hour" (12:27). "This hour" is the great crisis in the life of Jesus, the hour which no one could anticipate (7:30, 8:20), but from which, now that it has come, He will not shrink. It has come, in the sense already explained, as the hour in which the Son of Man is to be *glorified*, the hour in which He is to drink the cup which the Father gives Him to drink, and to crown the work the Father has given Him to do. The way in which He is moved by it, shrinks from it and accepts it, reveals the place it holds in His mind and in that of the evangelist also.[46]

Another allusion to the death of Christ as being both lifted up and glorified is to be found in 12:32-33, which reads: "And I, when I am lifted up from the earth, will draw all men to myself. He said this to show by what death he was to die." This and other passages (3:14; 8:28) are strongly suggestive of the cross. The act of Christ's dying is his glory, and he will thus be glorified forever. "There is no conception of a humiliation in death followed and rewarded by an exaltation. On the contrary, Christ is lifted up and ascends through His death. His glory is revealed in that whole experience which death initiates and into which it enters, more than in all His miracles."[47] The glorification of Christ is the sheer power of God to "draw all men to [himself]," that is, to raise all men to himself. John envisions the power of the cross drawing all men like helpless filings in a magnetic field.

Wherever one looks in the Gospel accounts, he cannot get past the necessity of death. Certainly, it was the necessity of the death of Christ that accounts for a "gospel" for the Gospels.

It is possible, however, to go further in defining the death of Christ in the fourth Gospel. Proceeding as it does from the love of the Father and the Son, it is nevertheless not conceived as arbitrary. It is free, but there is a rational necessity for it. The Son of Man *must* be lifted up if He is to save those who believe. The corn of wheat *must* fall into the ground and die if it is not to abide alone. Not much, indeed, is said to explain this. The various ends secured by Christ's death . . . [(10:11, 3:14ff., 11:52)] . . . these, no doubt, are all somehow dependent upon it. But just how, the evangelist is at no pains to tell. We do no violence to his thought, however, when we put this and that in the Gospel together in order to discern what he does not say explicitly.[48]

It is difficult to talk in terms of what death means for the individual because there are two factors that continually enter into the subject. One is the emphasis on the death of Christ; all its implications for us will meet our own specific needs. There is no reflection on the subject of death for the Christian apart from the death of Christ. The second aspect is that John is so motivated by the concept of Life or eternal life that he would rather hold before individuals the positive and attractive side of the question, especially because this Life can begin in the "here and now." The person who rejects the Life is one who turns from life to death, from light to darkness, from truth to error, and from "living water" to abject thirst. Thus, he who dies in this condition is without Life. He has turned from the riches and the fullness of what Christ has to offer. Death is the negation of Life. Man would rather stand with his sin than be redeemed.

But to St. John the world so regarded is the world of men alienated from God, blind to his presence, and hostile to his rule. He looks in one direction and sees Vanity Fair, with its cheap glitter and its empty pomps, its corruption and its disillusionment, and he foretells its swift decay. He looks in another direction, and he sees society organized in stark opposition to God, refusing to accept the freedom of the truth, resolutely bent upon the destruction of the Christian witness, and animated by hatred against Christ himself and all who make confession of his faith. . . . "To this end was the Son of God manifested, that he might destroy the works of the devil." St. John never leaves God out of account. The Gospel is the epic of the conflict between light and darkness, with its culminating intensity at the Cross. The Epistle carries on the tale as the struggle between the Church and the World. *Fides Victrix!*[49]

There are those who believe that the death of Christ does not take prominence in the Fourth Gospel as it does in the rest of the New Testament. Professor Denney wishes to put away their fears.

No doubt there is much in the fourth Gospel which makes it plausible to say, Paul deals with the work of Christ, John with His person; for Paul, Christ only lives to die; for John, He dies because death is the only issue from life; but such contrasts do as much to mislead as to illumine. As soon as we are past the prologue into the scenery of what Jesus actually said, did, thought, feared, and suffered, we see that His death really fills the place it does everywhere in the New Testament, and has the same decisive importance.[50]

Death permeates all the writings of John; it is the very antithesis of eternal life which John is striving to convey. "Death is thus a central feature of John's Son of man doctrine, but it will be remarked that for him the death of Jesus is at the same time his glory. . . ."[51]

"What John perceived with far greater clarity than any of his predecessors was that Jesus *is* the Gospel, and that the Gospel *is* Jesus. It was through the life, and especially through the death and resurrection, of Jesus that men had been admitted to the blessings of the messianic kingdom, and the highest blessing of that kingdom was, as Paul had already seen, the life of communion with Christ himself: 'for me, to live is Christ'

(Phil. 1:21). That is, when the Gospel was offered to men it was Christ himself who was offered to them, and received by them. It was intolerable therefore that the person of Christ should remain undefined. Paul, who had recognized the same truth, evidently felt the same obligation."[52]

Jesus' coming for man was not, in the sight of John, to establish a new morality or ethical aspect. It was man's means of salvation. "Salvation is the fruit of the whole incarnate life of Jesus Christ, including his death and resurrection; consequently it is revealed in all his actions. The miracles in particular show figuratively what salvation is—the curing of the sick, the feeding of the hungry, the giving of sight to the blind, and the raising of the dead. Salvation, that is, means the healing of the ills of mankind, and the imparting of light and life; in other words, Jesus deals with sin, and gives men knowledge and life. These aspects of salvation are seen from time to time in the course of the gospel, but appear pre-eminently in the death and resurrection of Jesus."[53]

This salvation opens an entirely new sphere of man's relationship to God. This is what the entire activity of Christ was about.

What men needed was to be sanctified, that is, to be consecrated to God. It was not in their power to consecrate themselves, and surely no reason can be conceived for this but that which lies in their sin. But what they were not able to do for themselves Christ did for them in His own person. He consecrated Himself to God in His death. That the reference is to His death does not seem open to question; the present tense, ἁγιάζω, which suggests something going on at the moment, and the circumstances of our Lord, whose mind as He speaks is full of what is at hand, put out of court the idea that the word is intended to describe His life as a whole. His life was past, and now, in His own person, through death, He is about to establish between God and man a relation which men could never have established for themselves, but into which they can truly enter and into which they will be drawn once it is established by Him. This seems to me the exact equivalent of the Pauline doctrine that Christ dies our death that we may be drawn into the fellowship of His death, and so put right with God. He acts—"I sanctify Myself"; men are acted on—"that they themselves also may be sanctified". He establishes the reconciliation; they, to use Pauline language, receive it (Rom. 5:11).[54]

The very act of Christ's death followed by the resurrection was an eschatological event opening, as it were, "the Way" for all succeeding eschatological activity. "His death was not a normal human fate but the death which God caused him to die for us. He did not deserve his death by his sin but was made a sinner for us by God and condemned as one (II Cor. 5:21; Rom. 8:3; Gal. 3:13f.); he died for us."[55] The details of the death and resurrection hold a special fascination for John. This in itself is curious, for he is able to fluctuate from universal concepts such as the Logos (the Word) to the specific detail of the grave clothes. Here is almost a breach with the exaltation of the Lord Jesus. Yet, John is not so quick to move from the historicity of Jesus as might be first imagined because of his lofty ideas.

The Gospels all emphasize the fact that the tomb in which Jesus was buried was found empty, and therefore by implication the physical resurrection of the Lord. St John (following St Luke) has also emphasized the matter by his elaboration of the detail of the grave-clothes (vv. 6 f.). There are no reasons whatever, either in modern science or in modern philosophy, why we should not accept the N[ew] T[estament] witness concerning the Empty Tomb. If we truly believe that God performed the stupendous act of raising Jesus from the dead, we will not quibble about how he could or could not have done it. The bodily resurrection of the Lord is theologically very important in shewing that the whole of creation is to be redeemed, the physical no less than the spiritual. Nevertheless, St John does not wish to leave us with the impression that the body of Jesus was entirely unchanged; it was the same body by which his disciples had always recognized him, the body which bore the marks of the nails and the spear; yet it was transformed, a glorified body, for Jesus had now ascended to the Father. As usual St John conveys deep theological truth in the form of a story. Jesus came and stood in the midst, in his resurrection body, although the doors were bolted FOR FEAR OF THE JEWS. Thus, the body of Jesus was now different in some respects from the body that hung on the cross; and yet it was the same body, for that was how the disciples knew who he was: HE SHOWED UNTO THEM HIS HANDS AND HIS SIDE (v. 20).[56]

The specific details considered here are a definite play to Hebrew thinking. For the Greek, they would have detracted from the pictures already illustrated by John.

Indeed, in the death of Christ John brings us closest to his humanity. Whatever else we may say of the death of Christ, it was sheer agony. "The 'Agony' is taken at this point not because John feared that such human anxiety would spoil the effect of ch. 17 but because in the present chapter he was summing up the ministry of Jesus in terms of service and death. No synoptic narrative better illustrates the devotion of one who hates his life in this world, and John's form of the story illustrates also God's strength made perfect in weakness; he thus presents the combined humiliation and glory of the earthly life of Jesus, both of which were to be consummated together in the cross."[57] Certainly it is at the cross where the two natures of Christ become most apparent in tension.

Jesus . . . groans "from grief and anger". . . . But if we reflect that our Lord's gaze was directed not only at the sign but at what it signified, not only at the immediate circumstances, the physical death and the tears shed for it, but at the infinitely greater tragedy of spiritual death, the infinitely greater horror of the evil which causes it and thereby causes also the immensity of the world's pain, the *lacrimae rerum,* the tears with which the whole world is drenched; and if we add to this our Lord's awareness that this sign would precipitate the final attack upon himself and so bring about his own death, and that when he was lifted up there would be some who would gaze at him, not lovingly, to receive life, but jeering at him in a final act of life-rejection—if we bear all this in mind it is indeed not unreasonable to suppose, as was suggested above, that our Lord's intense anger was directed against the dark mystery of evil—soon, now, to be referred to as the "Prince of this world" (12:31)—who is responsible in the last resort for all the vileness and treachery and cruelty, all the blindness and folly and futility, and all the appalling pain and misery, which darken the lives and the hearts of men.[58]

However difficult the agony may have been, it was not beyond the knowledge of God. "Even for Jesus obedience unto death is costly; but the cost, being expressed in the language of the Old Testament, does not lie outside God's calculation."[59] Professor Denney states that there is a particular thrust in the Passion story which emphasizes the aspect of death as a means of prophetic fulfillment and focuses on some of the unusual circumstances surrounding the account.[60]

The next important passage from which one can learn about John's concept of death is the account of the raising of Lazarus. This is the apex of miracle stories and is placed here to point to the fact that this is to be the precursor of Christ's own death. The stage is set, and the death and resurrection of Lazarus may well hasten the death of Christ. The background for the scene is the opportunity to discuss two different eschatologies. One is the current Jewish eschatology, and it is compared with the early Christian point of view. Both doctrines have been noted previously. There is a conscious effort to relate this account to an earlier saying (5:28-9). "Lazarus, unlike the dead persons raised to life in the Synoptic Gospels, is already in the grave, and unlike them he comes to life at the bare word of Jesus. It certainly appears as though the evangelist had deliberately dramatized the saying, 'Those who are in the tombs will hear His voice and come forth.' The miracle of Lazarus's bodily resurrection, which anticipates the final resurrection, is a symbol of the real resurrection by which a man passes from a merely physical existence, which is death, into the life which is life indeed, and which is proof against the death of the body."[61] This follows on the heels of the other miracle accounts, which are seen in increasing depth and trust—building into a great *crescendo*—affirming that you will ultimately trust Jesus in death as in Life, for he has become your Life. The weight and power of the account rest on the spoken word of Jesus. Does this not imply that at this point Jesus has truly reached the full implication of being the Word of God? If this is parallel to the creation account in Genesis, one sees that Jesus has manifested the dynamic, creative power which is accomplished through the spoken Word of God.

Following this same thought more closely, one finds that if he is receptive to the Word of God in the "here and now," he participates in the "resurrection-in-life." In 6:54 there is "a parallel to the pregnant use of 'life' in the sense of 'life of the Age to Come', which as we have seen occurs occasionally in the Talmud, with 'death' as its antithesis. But here the 'death' which is in view is rather the mode of existence of unenlightened, unredeemed humanity. . . . According to this conception the death of the body alone can release man from death into the life which is life indeed. But as we have seen, some of the Hermetic writings allow the possibility of beginning such a life here and now. For John this present enjoyment of eternal life has become the controlling and all-important conception."[62]

This life for the believer is a transcendent life. It escapes the various systems of time to make eternity operative today. "The thought of the Fourth Gospel has, as we have seen, some affinity with that of Philo. It appears that he too means by ζωή αἰώνιος 'eternal life' in the Platonic sense, at least so far, that it is a life not measured by months and years, a life which has properly speaking neither past nor future, but is lived in God's eternal To-day. To think of any end to such life would be a contradiction in terms. If therefore it is to be thought of in terms of time, that 'image of eternity' within which human experience lies, it must be thought of as everlasting."[63]

Apparently the physical reappearance of Lazarus could be misconstrued. The emphasis must fall on the sheer power of Life over death. Even though Lazarus was brought back from death, this was not the important thing; what was important was the quality of Life over against the quantity of life. The raising of Lazarus is a very dramatic way of reiterating the theme. "Jesus is the resurrection and the life; apart from him there is no resurrection and no life, and where he is, resurrection and life must be. Jesus is always the realization, in this world, of eternal life in the experience of Christians; in order that this truth may be manifested in a sign he accomplishes the resurrection of Lazarus."[64]

Much more emphasis is placed on the fact that Lazarus died than in similar healing accounts in the Synoptics. On this

score John leaves one with no doubts. " 'A state of death beyond the third day meant, from the popular Jewish point of
view, an absolute dissolution of life. At this time the face cannot be recognized with certainty; the body bursts; and the
soul, which until then had hovered over the body, parts from
it. . . .' "[65] According to traditional Hebrew belief, the soul
hovered over the body and then departed on the fourth day. A
period of three days or fewer constituted a temporary residence;
after four days it was considered a permanent residence. This
is why the New Testament church made a point of proclaiming
that Jesus arose on the third day. This indicates to all that the
tomb was only Jesus' temporary abode but also holds up the
fact that he died. In the Lazarus story Jesus waits until the
fourth day to attest to his death. Thus, John emphasizes the
stupendous nature of the miracle. If there had been misunder-
standings or doubts about the actual death in the Synoptic
accounts, this would alleviate all fears. This dramatic account
emphasizes the crisis and tension concerning death.

In one sense therefore the moment of death should seem of far
less importance to the christian than to the non-believer. But in
another sense it must be of far greater importance, since it is the
moment of ultimate *krisis* or decision upon which eternity hangs:
we pass judgement upon ourselves, and this is the moment at
which sentence is definitively pronounced. Yet here again we are
not to confuse religion with superstition: we are not to suppose
that after a lifetime of truly loving and devoted service of God
a man could in his last moments slip into some contravention of
the law which would nullify all his love and his goodness and
plunge him into hell. We shall die as we have lived—we shall be,
when death comes, what our way of life has made us—but with
one qualification of immense importance: it is superstition to suppose that a lifetime of love can be wiped out by a moment of
frailty; it is not superstition to believe that a lifetime of frailty
can be redeemed by a moment of love, for our Lord, in his words
to the "good thief" and his comment on the woman "who was a
sinner", tells us that this is so. Jesus is the Lord of life, physical
and spiritual, temporal and eternal; and when he speaks to Martha
of life and death it is with the life eternal that he is concerned.
Martha's appeal for his help has been couched in vague terms:

she has not formulated to herself the possibility of his raising Lazarus from the dead; when he tells her, "Your brother will rise again", she thinks he is referring to the resurrection at the end of the world; and even when he goes on to declare that he is resurrection, here and now, because he is life, he still does not announce his immediate purpose, the "sign", but states the ultimate reality to which that sign points: that those who believe in him shall never die, for already, here and now, they have triumphed over death in every sense of the word that really matters.[66]

Implicit in the resurrection of Lazarus is something of his personal nature. Either he was a man worthy of Life, or he had already begun to participate in the Life. Without this aspect or quality, this scene would be merely a demonstration. There is also a parallel here to the compassion of healing as demonstrated in the Synoptics. A part of the miracle was created out of compassion for Mary and Martha. Thus, Jesus responded once more to minister to the bereaved. Love must be the supreme motivation for all the miracles.

The conclusion of the story is not that Jesus brought one man back from the dead but rather that he will bring all back from the dead. This is the most significant "sign" in the entire "Book of Signs." "The truth of history is that Jesus was put to death not as a good man, a righteous prophet, a religious genius or an ethical teacher, but as the Son of God. Thus, the 'truth' of the Lazarus story is far greater than a literalistic, unimaginative reading of it could reveal: it concerns not the resuscitation of one dead man, out of all the millions of human dead, but the appearance in the history of this world of him who is the creator of life itself, Jesus the Son of God, *the* resurrection and *the* life."[67]

What, then, are the specific implications of the eschatological ideas, as they are presented in the concepts of Parousia, judgment, and the resurrection with the final consummation? The introduction of the word *Parousia* by John implies that he looks to an objective advent in the final day. "While 'John' was no doubt one of the Christians for whom some of the details in the Church's account of the Parousia, the 'last day', and the Last Judgement, were symbolic, he does not silently discard the belief in the event called the End, but it lays bare its spiritual basis. Here, while he had predecessors in Paul and the writer to the Hebrews, he is a consummator."[68]

R. H. Charles sees the Parousia as having "a twofold meaning, a spiritual and an historical, in St. John. Thus in John 14:18, 19 the coming Advent is resolved into . . . an event already present: 'I will not leave you desolate: I come unto you. Yet a little while, and the world beholdeth me no more; but ye behold me: because I live, ye shall live also.' Thus in a spiritual sense Christ is already present (1 John 5:12): 'He that hath the Son hath life.' A spiritual and an abiding communion is already established between the exalted Christ and His own (12:26): 'If any man serve me, let him follow me; and where I am, there shall also my servant be: if any man serve me, him will my Father honour.' "[69] Thus, John puts Christianity on a faith-union basis with himself and the Father. The paradox of John's writings is that they are written from two points of view with frequent alternation.

From a standpoint placed in the period of the ministry of Jesus, "the hour is coming"; from John's own natural standpoint within the life of the Church after the resurrection and Pentecost, "the hour now is". But this is only a partial explanation, for . . . the basis of John's thought is that true worship can exist only in and through Jesus, and that worship in and through him is true worship. Consequently it is correct to say that, wherever Jesus is, there worship in Spirit and truth is possible; but this possibility is necessarily qualified by a future, or its equivalent ("the hour cometh"), because, and as long as, the person of Jesus himself is qualified in this way: he is the Messiah and he will be the Messiah; he has come and he will come. The worship of Christianity is an anticipation of the worship of heaven, but it is not yet the worship of heaven.[70]

The implication of John 5:25 is not the same as that of John 5:28, nor is it an anticipation of chapter 11. Rather, John's mind is here captivated by the immediate present. "A different kind of death and resurrection, of which the death and resurrection of the body are a parable, is in mind. There is a sense in which the word of the Son of God in the present world brings to life those who are dead (cf. 11:25f.); the promise is already being fulfilled, but is being fulfilled in such a way as to leave over something of itself for a future fulfillment also."[71] This rule over men is simply by the power of love. Its parallel is found in Augustine's "dangerous doctrine" of love: "Love God and do as you please."

The futuristic portion of the Parousia doctrine is the drawing into closer proximity of God to his people. "Thus Christ will return from heaven and take His own unto Himself, that they may be with Him in heaven (14:2, 3). . . . According to the New Testament, death translates believers to Christ (2 Cor. 5:8; Phil. 1:23; Acts 7:59), but nowhere is He said to come and fetch them."[72] The apostle looks longingly toward the Parousia and hopes that he will be around long enough to see it. He thinks of it as almost a reward for a long and lengthy life of service. "Jesus proclaims the spiritual power of the *eschaton*, the final order, of the Kingdom which has already broken in. And this was a characteristic of his teaching which later tradition obscured. In Otto's own words: 'He is the eschatological Saviour. Only thus understood are all his deeds and words seen against their right background and in their true meaning. Directly or indirectly, they are all sustained by the idea of a divine power which breaks in *to save*. This idea has its immediate correlate in the new God whom he brings, the God who does not consume the sinner but *seeks* him; the Father God, who has *drawn near* to men out of his transcendence, who asks for a childlike mind and a childlike trust, who frees not only from fear of the devil but from all fear and anxiety, who fills the entire life with childlike freedom from care.' "[73]

The kingdom is viewed only in the fullest in the future according to Jesus. " 'But what distinguishes his eschatology from that which had preceded it is, on the one side, that he already lives in the present active miracle of the final age, that with clear vision he sees this as something which is already coming into being and growing up around him, He knows himself to be supported by his powers already pressing on as an advance guard, and by their support and inspiration he works and preaches. On the other side, by his works, speech, parables, charismatic conferring of power, he mediates to a circle of disciples following in his steps, a contact with this miracle of the transcendent as a personal possession.' This is what is meant by the now familiar term 'realized eschatology.' "[74]

The judgment, no longer seen as the great judgment scene, is updated to the here and now and "spiritualized," so to speak. The Light has already entered the world and the world can never be the same. John believed that judgment had already permeated the world. "Judgment is conceived by this evangelist as present and subjective and as future and objective. Judgment in the former sense is no arbitrary process, but the working out of an absolute law whereby the unbelieving world is self-condemned. For a man is justified or condemned according to the attitude he assumes to the light (John 3:19-21). . . ."[75]

Since the Light is Jesus, the personal relation with Christ determines one's destiny both now and in the future. "There is no more characteristic term in the Fourth Gospel than *Judgement*. The noun and the verb occur thirty-one times in the Gospel. Here again the prevalent use by the Evangelist may easily lead us to overlook such passages as John 5:21ff. This must be read in full, as it is the clearest evidence that can be adduced for the claim that there is a Johannine eschatology, and that it is an integral part of the Gospel."[76]

The believer is left in watchful and eager expectation, which makes him continually aware of being under judgment. "The eschatological appeal on the lips of Jesus in the earlier Gospels, as also in the Pauline letters, is a call to vigilance. 'Watch, for you know not the day nor the hour.' So in the Fourth Gospel, where the present judgement dominates the thought, we meet with the same note of urgency, though the form of the appeal is not the same. Crisis overshadows the world. Men must walk in the light before darkness overtakes them. Obedient response to Jesus in faith must be given now. G. K. Chesterton's prayer,

> From sleep and from damnation,
> Deliver us, good Lord!

sums up the challenge to watchfulness in the Synoptic and in the Johannine language."[77]

John's thinking on judgment is not far removed from the concept running through the whole New Testament, which could be stated as: "There is continual Judgement going on all the time in the sense that men are being divided into 'good' and 'bad'; for those who die before the Parousia there is a final judgement at the moment of death, both for good men and bad, in the sense that all are then sentenced, the first to bliss and the second to woe; for those who are alive at the Parousia the final sentence falls when Christ comes."[78]

As a man finds it within himself to be faithful and obedient to the love of God, he moves from darkness to light, from death to life, and from estrangement to wholeness. "Since this present self-executing judgment is coextensive with the entire human life, it follows that a man's character is the result of all this process in the past, and is, in fact, the verdict of God on man's conduct from first to last. His ultimate destiny has thus already been determined by his spiritual condition. Hence, from this standpoint the final judgment cannot be otherwise conceived than as the recognition and manifestation of judgment already exercised and consummated."[79]

The last aspect of this eschatological examination will deal with the resurrection and the final consummation. To be consistent with John's thought, Life is the gift of God, and thus death must be the gift of the demonic. Resurrection is to insure that those who have walked in Light continue to do so, that is, to overcome the darkness of the demonic. "Seeing, therefore, that the resurrection in the fourth Gospel is, spiritually conceived, synonymous with eternal life, and, historically conceived, is the essential fruit of eternal life, two conclusions naturally follow: (1) The believer cannot lose this spiritual resurrection life at death, but must enter rather on a fuller consummation of it. (2) Only the righteous can share in that resurrection life."[80]

There are two aspects of resurrection emphasized in the Gospel of John. One is that the resurrection will come individually, and the other that it will come at the last day. In 5:28-29 "both righteous and unrighteous are described as coming forth from the tombs, and the scene is depicted in the most materialistic form—in fact, it would be hard to find a more unspiritual

167

description of the resurrection in the whole literature of the first century A.D. These considerations are of themselves quite sufficient to render these verses questionable in a high degree; for their teaching is in glaring conflict with the fundamental conceptions of this Gospel."[81] Basically the Johannine teaching gives the impression that the resurrection comes immediately after death. This is to be followed by the consummation, in which everything will be complete. "But the final result of this daily secret judgment must one day become manifest; believers shall have boldness in the day of judgment (1 John 2:28, 4:17), for it can only be the recognition and manifestation of judgment already exercised. A man's attitude to Christ determines now, and will determine finally, his relation to God and destiny (3:18, 19; 9:39)."[82]

The end, then, of this light-giving, life-giving process is the final consummation to blessedness. "After the final judgment the present world will pass away (I John 2:17), and Christ will take His own to heaven—a state rather than a locality (14:2, 3): they are to be with Him where He is (12:26, 17:24). Eternal life—the resurrection life—is then truly consummated. Begun essentially on earth, it is now realised in its fulness and perfected. The faithful now obtain their 'full reward' (2 John 8). As 'children of God' they are, through enjoyment of the divine vision, transformed into the divine likeness (I John 3:2, 3)."[83]

In regard to the final state of man:

Though the Apostle does not present us with any fresh teaching touching Hades and hell, he furnishes us with principles which in themselves necessitate a transformation of the Judaistic views regarding these intermediate and final abodes of the departed. Thus, when he teaches that God so loved the world as to give His only Son to redeem it (John 3:16), that "God is love" (1 John 4:8), that He is light, and in Him is no darkness at all, then Hades, which is wholly under His sway, must be a place where moral growth is possible; and as for hell, the final eternal abode of the damned, such a conception is impossible in the cosmos ruled by the God of justice and love. Sin, according to the Johannine view, is the destroyer of all life—physical, spiritual, and ontological. Now, to check the ultimate effects of this process of destruction and preserve the sinner in a state of sin, in a state of ever-growing, ever-deepening sin, could in no sense be the work of God so conceived.[84]

The Letters

The teachings of John in the letters follow closely those presented in the Gospel. "The ideas and the characteristic forms of expression are the same in each. In each the central thought is *life*. In each this *life* is *life* in the largest sense, and is antithetical to *death* or to *perdition*. In each it is exhibited in essentially the same aspects and relations. In Christ's teaching the *life* has its source and its seat in the Father, and is given by the Father to the Son, so that it is *in* the Son and can be imparted by Him to men. So in John's teaching the *life* is the reality that is before all time and behind all phenomena. It is with the Father in the beginning, and is historically manifested in the Son, so that it has been seen and borne witness to."[85] This Life comes to us as the fulfillment of the promise of God. "And this is what he has promised us, eternal life" (1 John 2:25).

The letters of John cannot see the death of Christ apart from sin (1 John 1:7; 2:1-2, 12; 3:5; 4:10). "We see here that the whole person and work of Christ, His whole manifestation in the world, and in some signal way His death, are set in relation to sin. . . . Here as in the Gospel it is characteristic of the writer that his interest is in the end or result, the actual cleansing of the soul from sin. . . . If we walk in the light as God is in the light, the blood of Jesus His son continuously and progressively cleanses us from all sin: our sanctification is gradually achieved under its influence (1:7)."[86] Sin is here faced as a blunt reality—that which separates us from God. The restored relationship can be brought about only at the cost of the life of a living Savior.

This, however, is not the end of the story.

The New Testament writers, though they speak often of Christ's death, never think of a dead Christ. Their Christ is One who became dead and is alive for evermore, and in His immortal life the virtue of His death is present. He did something when He died, and that something He continues to make effective for men in His risen life: but there is no meaning in saying that by His death His life, as something other than His death, is "liberated" and "made available" for men. On the contrary, what makes His risen life significant and a saving power for sinners is neither more nor less than this, that His death is in it. It is the life of One who by dying has dealt with the fatal necessities of man's situation, and in doing so has given a supreme demonstration of His love.[87]

The activity of Jesus on our behalf places him as an *ilasmos*. "Now the idea of *ilasmos* or propitiation is not an insulated idea. There cannot, indeed, be any such thing. It is part of a system of ideas, which we have to reconstruct with the means at our disposal. It is related, for one thing, to the idea of sin. It is sin, according to the uniform teaching of the New Testament, which creates the necessity for it, and which is in some sense the object of it. In other words, sin is the problem with which *ilasmos* deals. John agrees with all New Testament writers in regarding sin as a problem. It cannot simply be ignored or suppressed. Something has to be done with it, and the effective something has been done by Christ the *ilasmos*."[88]

The whole relationship of Christ's death for mankind is seen only through the idea of a blood sacrifice. "All that is divine, all the moral order of the world, all that we mean by the law of God, has right done by it in the death of Christ. Sin, in that sense, is neutralized by the propitiation, and if men could enter into it, or if the benefit of it could come to them, sin would no more be a barrier to their fellowship with God. The propitiation would draw them to God, put them right with Him and, as it held their hearts more closely, would more effectually and thoroughly cleanse them from every taint of sin."[89] The primary factor is again, as we saw in the Gospels, man's acceptance of God. It is an act, once for all, completed in the fullest sense. Man's part is simply to accept and respond to this love of God.

The question then arises, What is the relation of the love of God to sin?

John rises above all comparisons to an absolute point of view at which propitiation and love become ideas which explain each other, and which have no adequate illustration apart from each other. He defines not only the propitiation by relation to love—"God Himself loved us and sent His son to be the propitiation for our sins" (4:10); he defines love by relation to the propitiation—"in this have we come to know what love is, that He laid down His life for us" (3:16). . . . If the propitiatory death of Jesus is eliminated from the love of God, it might be unfair to say that the love of God is robbed of all meaning, but it is certainly robbed of its apostolic meaning. It has no longer that meaning which goes deeper than sin, sorrow, and death, and which recreates life in the adoring joy, wonder, and purity of the first Epistle of John.[90]

Summary

It is readily seen that the eschatological terminology of the Johannine corpus is "loaded." These loaded terms convey the nuances by which the theology of John is expressed. No other New Testament writer was quite so quick to relate the whole of Christian thought to the Greek world. No other New Testament writer throws us quite so quickly into the tension of the "now is" and "is to come." This is not so surprising when we reflect that it was John who had a deep and abiding respect for the Word and the words of God.

To John, the Word of God is a dynamic, creative, life-giving, light-giving force which seeks out men in order that they might find a right relationship with God, and works to hold them there. Thus, it was John's high and holy thought that this same Jesus was not a word from God in the sense of an ongoing revelation; rather, Jesus was the very Word of God. Jesus as the Word was God's fullest and finest revelation.

John's theme is a constant; it is simply the love of God. Death can no longer remain an abstraction, for the love of God has made man's relation to death the most subjective element in the universe. John communicates with his reader such ultimate ideas as life and death, sin and righteousness, as all-inclusive terms. In these terms John found the task not of projecting Christians into the future but of making the future active and present in the daily activities of the church.

In the Apocalypse one finds himself immersed in a "new heaven" and a "new earth" in linguistic symbols. John's fundamental insights into the ends of history are operative in every age. Thus, one finds his message to be always contemporaneous with history. The symbolism of the symbols became more real than reality to John. The warp and woof of the symbolism is ancient, but from these threads and his unsurpassed skill, John weaves the glory and triumph of God in a pattern which is *sui generis*. John, who has seen the ultimate, testifies and proclaims that even though death may hold its sway, it is God who has won the battle.

John believes that all is owed in some fashion to the death of Christ, which he sees as the Lamb of God slain for man. To see Jesus in sacrificial Hebrew terminology is to see the ultimate display of God's love, the obedience of Jesus unto death, and the high moral aspect expressed through the free will of Jesus.

One finds that the core of John's theology in his Gospel deals with the imparting of eternal Life to man. Thus, the "resurrection-in-life" of which Jesus speaks takes place before death and is active in the "here and now." The importance of this gift is that it is operative in the active present, and any future realization of Life is contingent on one's response to the Life now. All Christian theology is related to this concept of Life. It is an all-inclusive term which is tied to the act of creation. Jesus not only possesses Life but also is the source of all Life.

The Good Shepherd account, coupled with the concept of the seed, which must be dissolved, points to the necessity of Christ's death. The Good Shepherd is "good" precisely because he is willing to give up his life not only for his own sheep but also for the "other sheep" so that there might be one flock. His "going down" is simply for the purpose of later being raised up, which is also true of the seed and the crop. The glorification of Christ is the sheer power of God to draw all men to himself.

It is difficult for John to focus directly on the concept of death other than in the context of the negation and rejection of Life. He believed that there is no reflection on the subject of death for the Christian apart from the death of Christ. John is so motivated by the concept of Life or eternal life that he holds before his readers basically the positive and attractive aspect of Life. Thus, death can be defined only in light of Life. One who rejects the Life is the person who turns from Life to death, from light to darkness, from truth to error, and from "living water" to abject thirst. Death permeates all John's writings because it is the very antithesis of Life which he is striving to communicate.

The judgment is no longer seen as the great trial scene. It is updated to the here and now or "spiritualized," so to speak. The Light has already entered the world, and the world can never be the same. John thought that the judgment had already permeated the world and is active today in the subjective sense. Since the Light is Jesus, the personal relation with Christ determines one's destiny both now and in the future. As man finds it within himself to be faithful and obedient to the love of God, he moves from darkness to light, from death to Life, and from estrangement to wholeness.

The doctrine of the resurrection is to bring those who have walked in Light back continually into the Light, that is, to overcome the darkness of the demonic. The implications of this spiritual resurrection are 1) the individual will not ultimately lose his Life at death and in fact will only then come to its consummation; and 2) those who have not participated in Life in the here and now will not share in it in the future. The end, then, of this light-giving, life-giving process is the final consummation to blessedness, which is to walk in the Light as Christ is in the Light and to have fellowship one with another.

Conclusions

In REGARD to the subject of this book, a New Testament study of death, several things must be said. Any concluding statements are of necessity part of *a* Christian answer and are not *the* Christian answer to death. The ideas emphasized in this presentation are the tools with which one must work to develop a doctrine of death. One must realize that each age will refashion these same materials in order to make them relevant for that time.

The first part of the answer which biblical literature declares is that man must die. It is absurd to affirm the resurrection of the dead on the one hand and then on the other hand maintain that the life of a Christian will not be broken by the power of death. The Christian concept holds that death is a prerequisite for resurrection. The Scriptures proclaim that there is nothing inherently immortal in man and thus the Christian cannot accept immortality. The Christian doctrine of death does not evade death, nor does it deny it. The Christian is led through death, not around it.

Any future existence is completely contingent upon God. It was God's nature which created the problem of the finality of death in the minds of the early Hebrews, and thus it is to God one must return to answer these probings. The extension of the nature of God and the increasing importance of the individual stimulated the quest for an existence of life after death. Biblical literature time and time again holds before man the call to

"Life." Beyond "Life" which is operative in the "here and now" there is absolutely no need for any further existence because man finds fulfillment in this life through God. Man cannot earn, buy, or in any sense deserve a future life; he is simply thrown into the Holy Love of God, which graciously bestows a further life for the individual. Truly this is the free gift of God. The doctrine of resurrection is fundamental to all Christian thinking because it is here only that theology can show forth the omnipotence of God and the finitude of man.

The Christian accepts "life-resurrected," i.e., a life which has been reconstituted from the power of total death over man. Implicit in this doctrine is continuity and radical discontinuity of the individual believer. Death is radical because it destroys man completely; he can never be the same. "Life-resurrected" is an entirely new creation on the part of the Father which recreates the essential "self." It is the "self" which gives to man continuity with his past. The participation in "Life-resurrected" in the "here and now" makes eschatology operative in our daily existence, and it is the only certain guarantee of recreated continuity. Man is thus given over to life or death in the present by his response to the "Life-resurrected." As a man becomes more and more one "with Christ," heaven, hell, and judgment move to the dim recesses of the stage of life which is lighted by the holiness of God's love.

It is through death only that the nature of God is fully revealed. Nowhere is God seen more clearly than in the face of death. He bids us not to evade death but to pass through its terror because Christ has gone before us, defeating evil and bringing man to an ever closer relationship to God. Nowhere is the compassion of the Father seen as clearly as in the accounts of Jesus' raising the dead because of his compassion for the bereaved. Truly this is the gospel within the Gospels.

Death has no answers. Death gives no answers. The Christian answer to death begins in life and must be answered out of life and with life in the eternal present. Death challenges the whole thrust of man's life, and thus our "saving" response must be to direct the whole thrust of "self" against the assault of death. The Christian neither denies nor belittles death but faces it as a reality and moves forward to it. The Christian shares this life not only with death but also with God, who is Life, Light, and Love. It is through this same God that life and death come to have meaning; neither life nor death has meaning without God. The church is faithful only when, in response to Christ's request, his death is remembered and proclaimed "until he comes."

Notes

1. The Concept of Death in the Synoptic Gospels

1. Reprinted by permission of Schocken Books, Inc. from *Eschatology: The Doctrine of a Future Life in Israel, Judaism, and Christianity* by R. H. Charles (New York: Schocken Books, 1963), pp. 364-65. Also by permission of A. & C. Black, the British publishers.

2. Ibid., p. 366.

3. Ibid., pp. 368-69.

4. C. Ryder Smith, *The Bible Doctrine of the Hereafter* (London: Epworth Press, 1958), p. 157. Quotations from this book are used by permission.

5. Ibid., pp. 166-67.

6. William Strawson, *Jesus and the Future Life* (London: Epworth Press; Philadelphia: Westminster Press, 1959), p. 71.

7. Ibid., pp. 71-72.

8. Werner Georg Kümmel, *Promise and Fulfilment*, trans. Dorothea M. Barton (London: S.C.M. Press; Naperville, Ill.: Alec R. Allenson, 1957), pp. 27-28.

9. Strawson, *Future Life*, p. 74.

10. Ibid., p. 81.

11. Ibid., p. 82.

12. Ibid., p. 84.

13. Ibid., p. 85.

14. Ibid., pp. 89-90.

15. Ibid., p. 89.
16. James Denney, *The Death of Christ* (London: Inter-Varsity Press, 1951), p. 18. Quotations from this book are used by permission of the publishers.
17. Strawson, *Future Life,* p. 92.
18. Charles, *Eschatology,* p. 377.
19. Denney, *The Death of Christ,* p. 23.
20. Ibid., p. 25.
21. Ibid., p. 27.
22. Strawson, *Future Life,* p. 93.
23. Ibid., p. 94.
24. Oscar Cullmann, *Immortality of the Soul or Resurrection of the Dead?* (New York: Macmillan, 1958; London: Epworth Press, 1959), p. 6.
25. Ibid., pp. 21-22.
26. Ibid., pp. 24-25.
27. Ibid., pp. 25-26.
28. Denney, *The Death of Christ,* p. 30.
29. S.G.F. Brandon, *Man and His Destiny in the Great Religions* (Manchester: Manchester University Press, 1962), p. 195. Quotations from this book are used by permission of Manchester University Press and by permission of the University of Toronto Press, the publisher in North America.
30. J. H. Leckie, *The World to Come and Final Destiny* (Edinburgh: T. & T. Clark, 1936), p. 147. Quotations from this book are used by permission.
31. Ibid., p. 150.
32. Ibid., pp. 151-52.
33. Ibid., pp. 152-53.
34. Ibid., pp. 155-56.
35. John Baillie, *And the Life Everlasting* (London: Oxford University Press, 1956), p. 136. Quotations from this book are used by permission. U.S. edition—New York: Charles Scribner's Sons, 1933, p .162.
36. Ibid., p. 137. U.S. edition—p. 163.
37. Ibid., p. 140. U.S. edition—p. 167.
38. Edward Langton, *Good and Evil Spirits* (London: S.P.C.K., 1942), pp. 256-57. Quotations from this book are used by permission.
39. Leckie, *The World to Come,* pp. 88-89.
40. Langton, *Good and Evil Spirits,* p. 262.

2. *The Concept of Death in the Pauline Letters*

1. S.G.F. Brandon, *Man and His Destiny in the Great Religions* (Manchester: Manchester University Press, 1962), p. 197.
2. J. N. Sevenster, *Paul and Seneca,* trans. Mrs. H. Meyer (Leiden, Netherlands: E. J. Brill, 1961), p. 75. Quotations from this book are used by permission.
3. Brandon, *Man and His Destiny,* p. 213.
4. Ibid.
5. Ibid.
6. Ibid., pp. 213-14.
7. Ibid., p. 215.
8. Sevenster, *Paul and Seneca,* p. 233.
9. Ibid., p. 236.
10. Ibid., p. 237.
11. Ibid., pp. 237-38.
12. Oscar Cullmann, *Immortality of the Soul or Resurrection of the Dead?* (New York: Macmillan, 1958; London: Epworth Press, 1959), pp. 10-11.
13. Sevenster, *Paul and Seneca,* p. 239.
14. James Denney, *The Death of Christ* (London: Inter-Varsity Press, 1951), p. 65.
15. Ibid., p. 68.
16. Ibid., pp. 69-70.
17. Ibid., pp. 72-73.
18. Ibid., p. 73.
19. Ibid., p. 75.
20. Ibid., p. 76.
21. Ibid.
22. H. Wheeler Robinson, *The Christian Experience of the Holy Spirit* (London: Harper & Brothers, 1928), p. 78, quoted in W. D. Davies, *Paul and Rabbinic Judaism* (London: S.P.C.K., 1948), p. 228.
23. William Manson, *Jesus the Messiah* (London: Hodder & Stoughton, 1943), pp. 123 f., quoted in Davies, *Paul and Rabbinic Judaism,* p. 229.
24. Davies, *Paul and Rabbinic Judaism,* p. 229. Original quotations from this book are used by permission.
25. Ibid., p. 237.
26. Ibid., pp. 283-84.
27. Ibid., p. 285.

28. Ibid., p. 290.
29. Ibid., p. 291.
30. Ibid., p .292, quoting Héring.
31. Ibid., p. 297.
32. C. A. H. Guignebert, *The Jewish World in the Time of Jesus,* trans. S. H. Hooke (London: Routledge & Kegan Paul, 1939), p. 118, quoted in Davies, p. 299.
33. Davies, *Paul and Rabbinic Judaism,* p. 302.
34. Ibid., pp. 303-4.
35. Ibid., p. 308.
36. Reprinted by permission of Schocken Books, Inc. from *Eschatology: The Doctrine of a Future Life in Israel, Judaism, and Christianity* by R. H. Charles (New York: Schocken Books, 1963), p. 452. Also by permission of A. & C. Black, the British publishers.
37. Davies, *Paul and Rabbinic Judaism,* p. 310.
38. R. Travers Herford, *The Pharisees* (New York: Macmillan, 1924), pp. 168-69. Used by permission.
39. Albert Schweitzer, *The Mysticism of Paul the Apostle,* trans. William Montgomery (London: A. & C. Black, 1931), pp. 54-59. Quotations from this book are used by permission.
40. Ibid., p. 62.
41. Ibid., p. 65.
42. Ibid., p. 67.
43. Ibid., p. 68.
44. Ibid., p. 76.
45. Ibid., p. 83.
46. Ibid., p. 90.
47. Ibid., p. 91.
48. Ibid., p. 93.
49. Davies, *Paul and Rabbinic Judaism,* p. 297.
50. Schweitzer, *Mysticism of Paul,* p. 95.
51. Ibid., pp. 96-97.
52. Ibid., p. 98.
53. Ibid., p. 116.
54. Ibid., p. 119.
55. Ibid., p. 125.
56. J. H. Leckie, *The World to Come and Final Destiny* (Edinburgh: T. & T. Clark, 1936), p. 161.
57. Ibid., p. 168.
58. Ibid., p. 169.
59. Ibid.

60. Ibid., pp. 172-73.
61. Ibid., p. 174.
62. Ibid., p. 181.
63. Ibid., p. 182.
64. H. A. A. Kennedy, *St. Paul's Conceptions of the Last Things* (London: Hodder & Stoughton, 1904), p. 110. Quotations from this book are used by permission.
65. Denney, *The Death of Christ,* p. 143.
66. Ibid., pp. 151-52.
67. Ibid., pp. 77-78.
68. Karl Barth, *The Resurrection of the Dead,* trans. H. J. Stenning (London: Hodder & Stoughton, 1933), p. 21. Quotations from this book are used by permission.
69. Ibid., p. 22.
70. Ibid., pp. 22-23.
71. Ibid., p. 107.
72. Ibid., p. 118.
73. Ibid., p. 128.
74. Ibid., p. 157.
75. Ibid., p. 161.
76. Ibid., p. 167.
77. Ibid., p. 177.
78. Ibid., p. 181.
79. Ibid., p. 185.
80. Ibid., p. 186.
81. Ibid., p. 201.
82. Charles, *Eschatology,* p. 452.
83. Ibid., p. 453.
84. Denney, *The Death of Christ,* p. 79.
85. Ibid., p. 83.
86. Ibid., pp. 83-84.
87. Ibid., p. 84.
88. Ibid., p. 86.
89. Ibid., p. 87.
90. Ibid., p. 89.
91. Ibid., pp. 89-90.
92. Ibid., p. 94.
93. Ibid., p. 97.
94. Ibid., p. 102-3.
95. Ibid., p. 104.
96. Ibid., p. 108.

97. Ibid., p. 109.
98. Ibid., p. 110.
99. Ibid., pp. 112-13.
100. Ibid., p. 113.
101. Ibid., p. 115.
102. Ibid., p. 116.
103. Ibid.
104. Ibid., p. 117.
105. Ibid., p. 118.

3. The Concept of Death in the Johannine Writings

1. C. K. Barrett, *The Gospel According to St. John* (London: S.P.C.K., 1958), p. 57. Original quotations from this book are used by permission.
2. Prof. James T. Cleland, Duke University.
3. James Denney, *The Death of Christ* (London: Inter-Varsity Press, 1951), pp. 146-47.
4. Austin Farrer, *A Rebirth of Images* (Glasgow: MacLehose and Co., 1949), p. 19.
5. Martin Kiddle, *The Revelation of St. John,* The Moffatt New Testament Commentary (New York: Harper & Brothers, 1940), p. xxxvi.
6. Reprinted by permission of Schocken Books, Inc. from *Eschatology: The Doctrine of a Future Life in Israel, Judaism, and Christianity* by R. H. Charles (New York: Schocken Books, 1963), p. 405. Also by permission of A. & C. Black, the British publishers.
7. Denney, *The Death of Christ,* p. 134.
8. Ibid., p. 154.
9. Ibid., p. 135.
10. Ibid., pp. 135-36.
11. Ibid., pp. 140-41.
12. Ibid., p. 146.
13. Ibid.
14. Ibid., pp. 146-47.
15. Ibid., p. 138.
16. Ibid., p. 137.
17. Charles, *Eschatology,* p. 406.
18. Stewart D. F. Salmond, *The Christian Doctrine of Immor-*

tality, 4th ed. (Edinburgh: T. & T. Clark, 1901), p. 343. Quotations from this book are used by permission.

19. Charles, *Eschatology,* p. 407.

20. Edward Langton, *Good and Evil Spirits* (London: S.P.C.K., 1942), p. 287.

21. Charles, *Eschatology,* pp. 408-9.

22. Langton, *Good and Evil Spirits,* pp. 287-88.

23. Charles, *Eschatology,* pp. 409-10.

24. Ibid., p. 410.

25. Ibid., p. 411.

26. Ibid.

27. Ibid., p. 412.

28. Denney, *The Death of Christ,* p. 139.

29. W. F. Howard, *Christianity According to St. John* (London: Gerald Duckworth & Co., 1943), p. 97. Original quotations from this book are used by permission. Secondary quotation from Law is from *The Tests of Life,* p. 56.

30. C. H. Dodd, *The Interpretation of the Fourth Gospel* (Cambridge: Cambridge University Press, 1953), pp. 147-48. Quotations from this book are used by permission.

31. Ibid., p. 148.

32. Salmond, *Christian Doctrine of Immortality,* p. 391.

33. Dodd, *Interpretation of the Fourth Gospel,* p. 364.

34. Rudolf Bultmann, *Life and Death,* Kittel's Bible Key Words (London: A. & C. Black, 1965), p. 75.

35. Ibid., p. 76. Used by permission.

36. Howard, *Christianity According to St. John,* p. 109.

37. Ibid., p. 112.

38. Charles, *Eschatology,* p. 426.

39. Salmond, *Christian Doctrine of Immortality,* p. 391.

40. Denney, *The Death of Christ,* p. 143.

41. Dodd, *Interpretation of the Fourth Gospel,* p. 366.

42. Ibid., p. 367.

43. Ibid., p. 368.

44. Denney, *The Death of Christ,* pp. 142-43.

45. Dodd, *Interpretation of the Fourth Gospel,* p. 372.

46. Denney, *The Death of Christ,* p. 143.

47. Ibid., p. 142.

48. Ibid., p. 146.

49. Howard, *Christianity According to St. John,* pp. 84-85.

50. Denney, *The Death of Christ,* p. 145.

51. Barrett, *Gospel According to St. John,* p. 60.
52. Ibid., p. 58.
53. Ibid., p. 67.
54. Denney, *The Death of Christ,* p. 148.
55. Bultmann, *Life and Death,* p. 93.
56. Alan Richardson, *The Gospel According to Saint John* (London: S.C.M. Press, 1959; New York: Macmillan, 1962), p. 210. Quotations from this book are used by permission of Macmillan.
57. Barrett, *Gospel According to St. John,* p. 354.
58. From *The Eagle's Word,* pp. 83-84, © 1961 by Gerald Vann, O.P. Quotations from this book are reprinted by permission of Harcourt Brace Jovanovich, Inc., and William Collins Sons & Co.
59. Barrett, *Gospel According to St. John,* p. 354.
60. Denney, *The Death of Christ,* pp. 144-45.
61. Dodd, *Interpretation of the Fourth Gospel,* p. 148.
62. Ibid., pp. 148-49.
63. Ibid., p. 150.
64. Barrett, *Gospel According to St. John,* p. 329.
65. Gustaf Dalman, *Jesus-Jeshua,* trans. Paul P. Levertoff (London: S.P.C.K., 1929), p. 220, quoted in Barrett, p. 335.
66. Vann, *The Eagle's Word,* pp. 81-82.
67. Richardson, *Gospel According to Saint John,* p. 134.
68. C. Ryder Smith, *The Bible Doctrine of the Hereafter* (London: Epworth Press, 1958), p. 210.
69. Charles, *Eschatology,* p. 420.
70. Barrett, *Gospel According to St. John,* p. 56.
71. Ibid., p. 57.
72. Charles, *Eschatology,* pp. 421-22.
73. Howard, *Christianity According to St. John,* p. 116. Secondary quotation from Rudolf Otto, *The Kingdom of God and the Son of Man,* trans. Floyd V. Filson and Bertram Lee Woolf (Surrey, England: Religious Tract Society, 1938), p. 107.
74. Entire quotation except last sentence from Otto, *The Kingdom of God,* p. 155. Last sentence—Howard, *Christianity According to St. John,* p. 117.
75. Charles, *Eschatology,* pp. 422-23.
76. Howard, *Christianity According to St. John,* pp. 112-13.
77. Ibid., p. 120.
78. Smith, *Doctrine of the Hereafter,* p. 210.
79. Charles, *Eschatology,* p. 424.
80. Ibid., p. 428.

81. Ibid., pp. 428-29.
82. Ibid., p. 430.
83. Ibid., pp. 430-31.
84. Ibid., p. 431.
85. Salmond, *Christian Doctrine of Immortality,* p. 389.
86. Denney, *The Death of Christ,* p. 149.
87. Ibid., pp. 149-50.
88. Ibid., p. 150.
89. Ibid., pp. 150-51.
90. Ibid., pp. 151-52.

Bibliography

Baillie, John. *And the Life Everlasting.* London: Oxford University Press, 1956; New York: Charles Scribner's Sons, 1933.

Barrett, C. K. *The Gospel According to St. John.* London: S.P.C.K., 1958.

Barth, Karl. *The Resurrection of the Dead.* Translated by H. J. Stenning. London: Hodder & Stoughton, 1933.

Brandon, S.G.F. *Man and His Destiny in the Great Religions.* Manchester: Manchester University Press, 1962.

Bultmann, Rudolf. *Life and Death.* Kittel's Bible Key Words. London: A. & C. Black, 1965.

Charles, R. H. *Eschatology: The Doctrine of a Future Life in Israel, Judaism, and Christianity.* New York: Schocken Books, 1963.

Cullmann, Oscar. *Immortality of the Soul or Resurrection of the Dead?* New York: Macmillan, 1958; London: Epworth Press, 1959.

Davies, W. D. *Paul and Rabbinic Judaism.* London: S.P.C.K., 1948.

Denney, James. *The Death of Christ.* London: Inter-Varsity Press, 1951.

Dodd, C. H. *The Interpretation of the Fourth Gospel.* Cambridge: Cambridge University Press, 1953.

Farrer, Austin. *A Rebirth of Images.* Glasgow: MacLehose and Co., 1949.

Herford, R. Travers. *The Pharisees.* New York: Macmillan, 1924.

Howard, W. F. *Christianity According to St. John.* London: Gerald Duckworth & Co., 1943.

Kennedy, H.A.A. *St. Paul's Conceptions of the Last Things.* London: Hodder & Stoughton, 1904.

Kiddle, Martin. *The Revelation of St. John.* The Moffatt New Testament Commentary. New York: Harper & Brothers, 1940.

Kümmel, Werner Georg. *Promise and Fulfilment.* Translated by Dorothea M. Barton. London: S.C.M. Press; Naperville, Ill.: Alec R. Allenson, 1957.

Langton, Edward. *Good and Evil Spirits.* London: S.P.C.K., 1942.

Leckie, J. H. *The World to Come and Final Destiny.* Edinburgh: T. & T. Clark, 1936.

Richardson, Alan. *The Gospel According to Saint John.* London: S.C.M. Press, 1959; New York: Macmillan, 1962.

Salmond, Stewart D. F. *The Christian Doctrine of Immortality.* 4th ed. Edinburgh: T. & T. Clark, 1901.

Schweitzer, Albert. *The Mysticism of Paul the Apostle.* Translated by William Montgomery. London: A. & C. Black, 1931.

Sevenster, J. N. *Paul and Seneca.* Translated by Mrs. H. Meyer. Leiden, Netherlands: E. J. Brill, 1961.

Smith, C. Ryder. *The Bible Doctrine of the Hereafter.* London: Epworth Press, 1958.

Strawson, William. *Jesus and the Future Life.* London: Epworth Press; Philadelphia: Westminster Press, 1959.

Vann, Gerald. *The Eagle's Word.* New York: Harcourt Brace Jovanovich, 1961.